CAN WE AGREE TO DISAGREE?

Exploring the differences at work between Americans and the French: A perspective on the cultural gap, and tips for successful and happy collaborations.

Agathe Laurent & Sabine Landolt

TBR Books
New York

Copyright ©2020 by Agathe Laurent et Sabine Landolt

All rights reserved. No part of this publication may be reproduced, distributed, or transmitted in any form or by any means, without prior written permission.

TBR Books is a program of the Center for the Advancement of Languages, Education, and Communities. We publish researchers and practitioners who seek to engage diverse communities on topics related to education, languages, cultural history, and social initiatives.

TBR Books / CALEC
750 Lexington Avenue, 9th Floor
New York, NY 10022

www.tbr-books.org | contact@tbr-books.org

Front Cover Illustration © Bayrol Jimenez

ISBN 978-1-947626-48-5 (paperback)
ISBN 978-1-947626-49-2 (hardcover)
ISBN 978-1-947626-51-5 (eBook)
ISBN 978-1-947626-55-3 (paperback Premium)
ISBN 978-1-947626-56-0 (hardcover Premium)
Library of Congress Control Number: 2020938726

"To our American and French friends who have helped us become who we are, and have shaped how we think, making us curious about others and more open to differences."

"To our parents, who taught us since our very first day that every person, of any age, gender, color, social level, and nationality, is worth it."

CONTENT

Preface	10
About this book	13
TOPICS	15
Work... what for?	17
The thinkers and the doers	25
Socializing at work	31
The art of written messages	39
Meetings	45
Positive spirit versus critical mindset	51
Professional Relationships	59
Team – One for all and all for one?	65
The meanings behind the words	71
Did you say expertise?	79
Work styles and social codes of conduct	85
Give feedback – But how?	91
The do's and don'ts – The taboos	99
Conclusion	106
Appendix	108
About the authors	110
Artworks credits	112
Contributors and thank you	113
Why they like the book	114
About TBR Books	118
About CALEC	120

PREFACE

Who has never said or thought, "I do not understand what (s)he means; (s)he seems to understand nothing, the message has been lost!" These moments of discouragement are followed by a judgment — often negative: "they are all like this or that; they are stupid; they are crazy!"

All these reactions are very human and natural because, regarding cultural differences (or even any kind of difference), we all have the tendency to take refuge in what reassures us the most: our own point of view and our experience on how to work and live.

This book is born from 50 interviews of French and American individuals working with the other culture; all are true cases. You will read in these pages the experiences of people who, like you, live Franco-American relations with its frustrations, misunderstandings, and successes.

I interviewed Sabine and Agathe to ask them how they had experienced this book-writing and their collaboration. Sabine is Swiss and American, and she has also lived in Italy and in France. Agathe is French and has been living in the U.S. for many years, including in her early childhood. She has always worked internationally. They bring together all the complexity of their individual and collective multicultural work.

Both Sabine and Agathe also had challenging work-related experiences while living abroad. They told me that they have "cried in the toilets" and felt alone multiple times during their professional life, overwhelmed by their misunderstandings with their teams. What was their secret to succeeding, and what recipe did they use to work together with respect for their individual differences? Both cite an ability to step back and "start from a blank page" when a relationship begins to become tense due to mutual misunderstandings. Their curiosity and a genuine desire to learn constitute the wealth of motivation and positive energy needed to support taking a step back: an energy-consuming activity.

Indeed, to judge, to put the other in a box, or to use stereotypes, are very human solutions that we spend less energy on because it is so much easier and immediate!

But this also has the risk of locking us into our golden cage, going around in circles with the same ideas and confirming beliefs that may not be completely true. And, most importantly, it prevents us from enjoying the country we live in, enriching ourselves, and doing enough to create a unique combination of our culture of origin and the one of the host countries.

Sabine and Agathe also cite the ability to be surprised and to have a fresh look at the other, and not taking oneself too seriously, as essential qualities to survive the dreaded but often unavoidable cultural occurrence of being "lost in translation."

They say that what allowed them to move forward in the inevitable situations of great intercultural loneliness was to realize that, thanks to their differences, they possessed a real added value. "This book has been a kind of cathartic therapy! I finally put on paper the 'why' of all my efforts... it's good!" The collaboration of Sabine and Agathe, who could not be more different from each other, to write this book is the living proof that it is possible to overcome the differences to create, innovate, be surprised and have fun!

I am sure that this rich content will awaken a cultural reflecting pool where you will identify with positive and negative emotions. I invite you to read this book with openness. Its goal is to make you want to understand the other in order to improve your relationships at work and in your personal life. Like Sabine and Agathe, stay connected to your own humanity, with all its imperfections, and look at each other with humility and curiosity, two key qualities to succeed in any culture.

Have a good reading!

Anna

Anna Gallotti is a Global Executive coach who works with top-level decision makers around the globe.

ABOUT THIS BOOK

This book is not trying to reinvent the wheel nor digging into the "whys": We know there is a lot out there on its topic. What makes this book different is that, through real experiences, we can grasp the intensity of the pertinent emotions and measure the reactions.

This book shows the profound risk of mutual misjudgment.

This book is not trying to be scientific or theoretical—we know there are nuances among people, across regions, and through industries. A French person coming to the U.S. as an expat for a few years will not approach working with Americans in the same way as a French entrepreneur would. And it is the same for Americans moving to France. Moreover, there are also deep regional differences: working in NY is not the same as working in Dallas or Memphis, and France being very centralized, working in Paris or in a province outside is different too.

This book is about real stories, which we hope will make you smile and relate to, whomever you are and wherever you live.

This book is not trying to be comprehensive—the topics that we have gathered come directly from the 50 interviews—25 Americans and 25 French, conducted in a semi-directed mode, following the methods of Freud and Piaget, working with associations and spontaneous probes.

This book speaks about what matters most to people we interviewed, and where the issues are the most numerous.

This book is not about defending one perspective, nor about bashing—on the contrary. Our profound motivation is to provide a blueprint for a successful collaboration between Americans and the French. We know that both possess unique assets that can create an extraordinary alchemy.

This book provides tips and tricks on how to get there.

CAN WE AGREE TO DISAGREE?

In my company, we offer generous holiday packages. But that's not what gets American colleagues excited. They are more interested in money than in free time, especially since they have no social safety net. As a result, it is difficult to recruit. We hire other nationalities.

WORK... WHAT FOR?

Dans ma boîte, on offre des packages de vacances importants — mais ce n'est pas ce qui les fait triper. Ce qui les intéresse, c'est l'argent et pas forcément le temps libre. Logique, pour eux, c'est sans filet social! Du coup on a du mal à recruter. Alors on prend d'autres nationalités.

— **CLÉMENT, French**
   Spirits Industry, New York, U.S.

LIVE TO WORK   WORK TO LIVE

The Situation

Work is a key factor in the American self-identity. Because Americans have very little governmental support in case of emergencies, work is a critical means of survival for them. More importantly, Americans work continuously, with only short periods of breaks. Because they have less vacation, most of the workforce tries to shorten their days in order to sustain such a rhythm. This continuous presence at work contrasts drastically with the French way of working, which appears quite fragmented.

In France, workdays are longer and more intense: many French people leave the office later. Therefore lunch breaks are important, and part of the habits, as a means to refresh and reset for the afternoon. Also, unlike Americans, the French take time off more frequently to go on vacation and explore the world, as the system enables them to have paid time off. They like to recharge their batteries during these moments and feel they need time off to stay creative in their work.

At the end of the day, both, Americans and French work a lot, but this difference in rhythm leads to a lot of judgement from both groups, and sadly, the "clichés" in this matter are still deeply anchored.

Tips And Tricks

For Americans:
- Don't give into the stereotypes! The French are incredibly productive and work a lot too.
- Don't schedule your meeting with a French colleague during lunchtime as you might see resistance!
- Accept that the French need some time *off* to recharge, and let the work speak for itself.

For the French:
- Be sympathetic to Americans' fixation with their jobs: it is culturally reinforced and, for many, absolutely necessary for their safety and stability.
- Find a compromise: you may not see eye-to-eye on the French way of working, but overall you want to make it work too.
- Do not disconnect completely during your vacation as this could alienate your American colleagues: technology makes it easy to check in and make things move along smoothly without altering your time off.

In this situation, you might feel…

Aggressivity

Misunderstanding

Frustration

Impatience

Judgement

Paranoia

My parents taught me that to *work is to feed your family*. I tell the same to my kids. We have to work and unfortunately, sometimes, it can feel like life is not about enjoyment.

— MATT, American
Sciences, IL, U.S.

In my opinion, for the French, work is much more about being happy. You do not need to continuously climb up the corporate ladder and change jobs all the time. When I used to work with French people, that's what I learned from them... Sometimes I miss that now.

— ROBERT, American, 10 years in France
Health Industry, MA, U.S.

I went to Paris to meet the team in France. The social atmosphere there is very different! Colleagues are super serious and focused, but then everyone takes a break for lunch. I was so lost.

— SURYA, Indian American
Fashion Industry, CA, U.S.

> Je n'ai jamais le temps de déjeuner. On ne se pose même pas la question, on dispose de toi. On a des agendas partagés et on te met des meetings tout le temps. L'efficacité c'est ça. Donc je bouffe devant tout le monde. Le paquet de chips en réunion, pas le choix. C'est *get the job done*.[1]
>
> — CLÉMENT, French
> Spirits Industry, New York, U.S.

> Moi je n'arrive plus à bosser avec des Français. Les Américains, même avec un *rythme de diesel* c'est plus puissant. Ils ne s'arrêtent jamais. Les Français ne comprennent pas et veulent encore déconnecter deux semaines de suite, ça, c'est ingérable.[2]
>
> — THOMAS, French entrepreneur
> Tech. Industry, New York, U.S.

> Vive les 35 heures! Tout le monde quitte le bureau à l'heure. Moi, je suis la seule Américaine et je quitte le bureau quand mon boss me dit que je peux partir. Suis-je trop carriériste?[3]
>
> — JAIMEE, American, living in Paris
> Tech. Industry, Paris, France

[1] *I never have time for lunch. No one even questions it. You are at our disposal. We have shared agendas and you're put into meetings all the time. That is efficiency. Therefore, I eat in front of everyone. Eating chips in a meeting, not by choice. It's to* get the job done.

[2] *I can't work with French colleagues anymore. The Americans, even with a diesel-powered speed, are more powerful. They never stop. The French don't understand. They still want to stay screen-free for two weeks in a row, this is not manageable.*

[3] *Long live the 35 hours! Everybody leaves the office on-time. I'm the only American here and I leave the office when my boss tells me I can leave. Am I too career-oriented?*

THE THINKERS AND THE DOERS

In my opinion, the French over-complicate the work. I am very solution-oriented so it can be hard for them. To me, what's important is the agenda and the decisions! I noticed that the French also bring emotions to the table, which can be quite an issue too.

— SAMANTHA, American
  Luxury Industry, New York, U.S.

In this situation,
you might feel...

Frustrations
Confusion
Depreciation
Inefficiencies
Pressure
Lack of trust
Disengagement

A CULTURE OF ANALYSIS

A CULTURE OF ACTION

The Situation

When it comes to work, the French are known to be analytical and passionate. This style is most evident within their approach to decision-making. For the French, it is a priority to analyze every option and opinion, to ensure the ultimate course of action. The French want to prevent any mistake and like to plan way ahead to keep things under control. This makes them also very creative.

The American way is quite the opposite: their approach to decision-making mirrors the fast-paced American business. They focus on creating momentum and getting things done, while keeping their emotions in check. For Americans, testing and learning is okay, making mistakes is part of the process and not a shame, and adjusting on the go is not an issue but a necessity. These very different workstyles may frustrate. Too slow! Too rushed! Not well thought out! Just pragmatic and opportunistic for others.

Tips and tricks

For the French:
- You do not need to gather all opinions before deciding: there is always time for adjustments.
- Do not be afraid to make mistakes.
- Explore how you can leverage Americans' instinct and reactivity: it's one of their core assets and it can be very powerful.

For the Americans:
- Understand that the French are taught to be analytical and critical.
- Be patient.
- Allow more time for discussion and reflection before making decisions.
- Lean in on their ability to go deeper: this will help you make stronger decisions!

We sent a question to our French team and they did not reply as quickly as we would have liked. They were simply waiting to have all the answers, to give us a perfect answer. This delay almost made us lose our client! Americans always entertain the client by responding with whatever nuggets of information they have, even if they do not have all the answers.

— TED, American
FMCG Industry, New York, U.S.

On faisait toujours des SWOT quand j'étais encore en Europe. Mais depuis que je suis en Amérique, j'ai compris. On ne fait plus ça, on fait des SO: les *Strengths & Opportunities*! En fait, ça suffit et ça dit tout![1]

— NICOLAS, French
Luxury Industry, New York, U.S.

J'adore cette culture de l'action. Efficacité anglo-saxonne! La langue anglaise conduit la logique et le raisonnement.[2]

— LOUIS, French
Health Industry, MA, U.S.

Ça va très vite aux U.S. Par exemple, j'ai créé un *task force* sur le CSR. On s'est lancé et en fait, on ne savait plus ce qu'on voulait faire. Au départ, cela paraissait du *B.S.*, mais en fait, ce n'est pas grave. On voulait créer un momentum et maintenant on se pose la question plus sérieusement de ce qu'on peut faire. Et du coup, ça bouge, on avance.[3]

— MARC, French
Luxury Industry, New York, U.S.

Every time we do a presentation in the office, we notice how different the French are. We always start with the findings, whereas the French need to understand how we got there. We take this as a lack of trust on their part. On the whole, we hate to waste time demonstrating the thought process that leads to the findings—we feel like, *what's the point?*

— RYAN, American
Spirits Industry, New York, U.S.

---

[1] *We were still doing SWOT when I was in Europe. But since I've been in America, I've figured it out. We don't do that anymore, we do SO: Strengths & Opportunities! In fact, that's enough and that says it all!*

[2] *I love this culture of action. Anglo-Saxon efficiency! The English language drives logic and reasoning.*

[3] *Things are moving very fast in the U.S. For example, I created a task force on CSR. We got into it and, in fact, we didn't know what we wanted to do anymore. At first, it sounds like B.S. but in fact, it's ok. We wanted to create momentum and now we're really trying to figure out what we want to do. What is really great, is that it is moving forward.*

For example, birthdays. It's unbelievable! As you arrive in the morning at the office, everything is entirely decorated, balloons are flying everywhere. Someone came and did everything as a surprise. We blow out the candles with you, it's a crazy thing to do. The Americans really know how to be thoughtful! Celebrating important events in such an organized way is quite an art.

SOCIALIZING AT THE WORKPLACE

Par exemple, les *birthdays*… C'est incroyable ! Tu débarques le matin, ton bureau est entièrement décoré, les ballons volent partout. Quelqu'un est venu et a tout fait par surprise. On souffle les bougies avec toi, c'est un truc de fous. Comme ils savent être chaleureux, les Américains ! Célébrer les événements importants de manière si organisée, est tout un art.

— DELPHINE, French
  Beauty Industry, New York, U.S.

COLLECTIVE SOCIALIZATION
Planned

INDIVIDUALIZED SOCIALIZATION
Unplanned

The Situation

Americans have a culture of collective celebrations. This starts from school where the kids celebrate all type of events and achievements. This culture continues into to college, in sports and also at home. Thus, they also love to plan social events at work and find every occasion to do so.

In contrast, the French do not have such culture. They value more personal and individualized relationships. They favor deeper and more intimate occasions to show their consideration and interest in others. They may find those frequent celebrations and office traditions kind of time-consuming. Americans won't understand their reserve or even their potential distance in these moments.

Tips and tricks

For Americans:
- Accept that the French need a more intimate way to engage in relationships.
- Do not get offended if you sometimes notice that your French colleague do not join every single office celebration.
- Don't do this end of day when the French want to go home, but rather before (apero) or after lunch (coffee).

For the French:
- Let it go: Even if you don't understand, it is interesting to embrace these moments as they say a lot about the American culture and ways Americans interact with each other.
- Enjoy these collective moments of celebration. They are unique for creating a team culture.
- Learn to have fun at the office.

In this situation,
you might feel…

Isolation

Mismatch

Discomfort

Disconnection

Frustration

Mon équipe est jeune, on organise tout le temps des trucs. L'autre jour ils me parlaient du *Pie day*... Chacun amène une tarte. Donc moi aussi, j'amène une tarte. Mais je n'avais rien compris. *Pie day* c'était pour le chiffre *PY* ! On a passé l'après-midi à manger des tartes et à rigoler, et moi je me disais qu'ils cherchent vraiment tous les prétextes pour s'amuser.[1]

— DELPHINE, French
Beauty Industry, New York, U.S.

During my stay in Paris, I had lots of one-on-one lunches. You don't talk business during lunch, instead, you create connections that go beyond your working relationship and leave the work at the office. Once back at the office, everyone goes back to their desk, just like nothing happened. This was fascinating to me!

— HELEN, American
Hospitality Industry, London, U.K.

La première année, j'étais sidérée. Chaque semaine il y avait des trucs — le *bring your kids/office day*, ou le *bring your pets day*, ou le *dress in blue day*. Les vendredis, on fêtait les gros deals. C'était du non-stop, il fallait tout le temps organiser et planifier les fêtes. Après je me suis habituée, mais pour moi, c'était une vraie perte de temps.[2]

— NADINE, French
Finance, New York, U.S.

[1] My team is very young, we're always organizing stuff. The other day, they were telling me about Pie Day. Everyone brings a pie. I'm bringing a pie as well. But I didn't get it at all. Pie day was for the number pi! We spent the afternoon eating pies and laughing, and I thought… you know what? They are really looking for every excuse to have fun.

[2] The first year, I was stunned. Every week there was something going on—the bring your kids to office day, or the bring your pet day, or the dress in blue day. Fridays, we celebrate the big deals. It was non-stop, you had to plan and organize parties all the time. Afterwards I got used to it, but for me, it was a real waste of time.

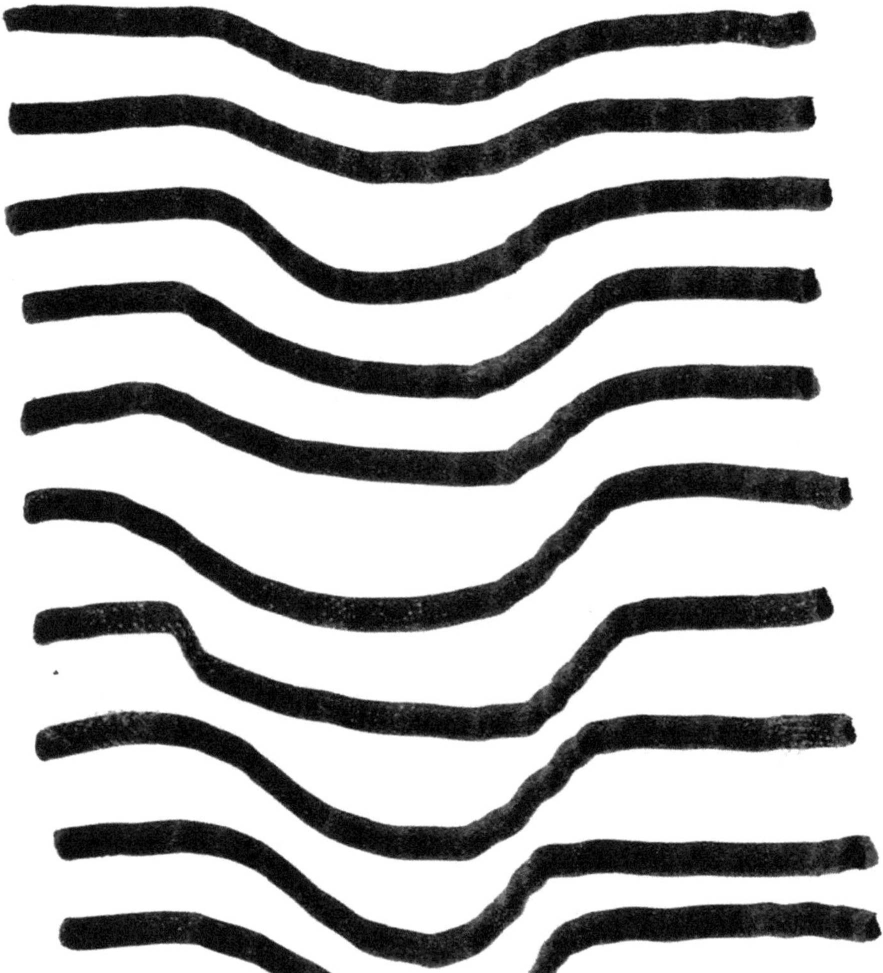

THE ART OF WRITTEN MESSAGES

Talking to French colleagues, I realized that a one-line email is seen as extremely rude. However, this is quite a common practice in the U.S.; we don't mean to be impolite, we just want to be efficient, so we focus on what's key.

— SARAH, American
　Finance, New York, U.S.

CONCISE AND TO THE POINT

ARTICULATE AND CONSIDERATE

The Situation

Americans write short emails and their messages are brief. Their priority is to get things done quickly and efficiently. They don't waste time with formalities and go to the point.

In contrast, the French consider formalities as a sign of respect. They pay attention to the codes of written communication (e.g., say hello, ask how the person is doing, etc.). For them, it is viewed as rude to receive an email purely as a transactional communication.

Tips and Tricks

For Americans:
- Understand that the French expect some formalities.
- Start your emails with a personal touch; you don't want to be seen as a rude person.
- Show your consideration by elaborating your messages a little more.

For the French:
- Don't take offense if the American communication style is straight to the point. It doesn't mean that they don't value your work nor care about you.
- Skip the formalities when engaging with Americans; they do not require them!
- Time is money in the U.S., so try to answer concisely and quickly.

In this situation,
you might feel…

Disrespect

Offence

Inefficiency

Annoyance

Judgement

The French are very formal with their emails. It always takes me a while to email the French team in Paris because I really have to think it through when I need to ask for something. In the U.S. we just say *Hi Samantha*! We make it short and direct. But in France, they use *Bonjour Monsieur/Madame* and always inject much longer sentences. I still struggle to understand why it matters!

— SAMANTHA, American
Luxury Industry, New York, U.S.

Je suis toujours très surpris lorsque je reçois des emails qui ne commencent même pas par me demander comment je vais. Je pense honnêtement qu'ils pourraient faire un peu plus attention, car cela parait très abrupte ![1]

— PIERRE, French
Finance, IL, U.S.

Typing an email is a whole issue to the French. I remember a time when I had to ask a very simple question and it took me ages to write an email that was formal enough. I know I have to pay a lot of attention and elaborate more rather than send out something concise.

— JENNIFER, American
Food Industry, New Jersey, U.S.

Les Américains se fichent des formalités ! Ils envoient des emails et s'attendent à ce que vous leur répondiez immédiatement. Je prends toujours le temps de lire et de réfléchir à ce que je dis avant de l'envoyer, en m'assurant toujours d'être polie, même après vingt ans dans ce pays ![2]

— NATHALIE, French, 20 years in the U.S.
FMCG Industry, IL, U.S.

[1] *I'm always very surprised when I get emails that don't even begin with a How are you? I honestly think they could be a little gentler because it sounds very abrupt!*

[2] *Americans don't care about formalities! They send emails and expect you to answer them immediately. I always take the time to read and to think about what I say before sending, always making sure to be polite, even after twenty years in this country!*

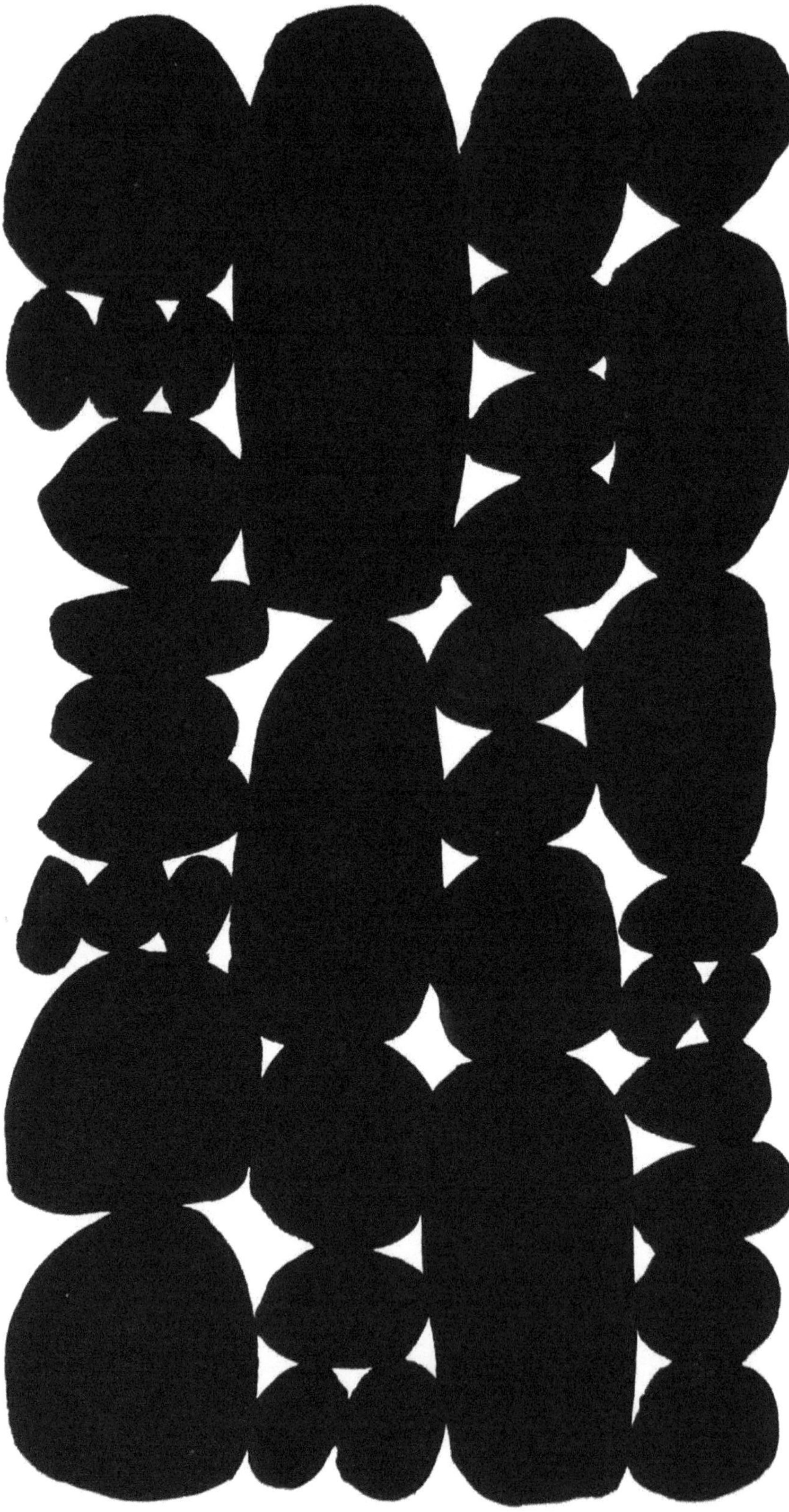

MEETINGS

Aux USA, la réunion démarre à l'heure, sur les cinq sujets évoqués, trois au moins seront réglés voir plus, et c'est bien comme ça. En France, on va jusqu'au bout de tout, on passe tout en revue, et on déborde à chaque fois, et du coup il faut une autre réunion pour continuer !

— CLÉMENT, French
   Spirits Industry, New York, U.S.

In the U.S., the meeting starts on time, out of the five topics discussed, at least three of them will be covered or even more, and that's good. In France, we go so deep on everything, we go over and overflow each time, so we need another meeting to continue!

ACTION-ORIENTED
Leave with a plan!

DISCUSSION-ORIENTED
Leave with another meeting!

The Situation

Americans are get-down-to-business people who favor clear-cut agendas. They define ownership and action plans as criteria for successful meetings, and are protective of their time. In the U.S. productivity is the priority. Above all else, Americans are focused on the work itself.

In contrast, the French see meetings as an opportunity for establishing connections with people. They approach meetings in a less structured way, allowing the conversation to flow, new topics to emerge and leave space for the human connections. This often means, they are open to follow up meetings if necessary.

For Americans, this feels extremely inefficient and lacks a certain level of seriousness, while for the French, the American way of organizing meetings may seem very robotic.

Tips and Tricks

For Americans:
- Involve your French teammates in deciding the meeting agenda.
- Be flexible and allow the conversation to be fluid: sometimes it is needed.
- Remember that meetings can be valuable in different ways, beyond just being productive.
- Make some time for building connections too!

For the French:
- Learn to prepare agendas, to set a purpose and/or objective for the meeting: your American colleagues need this structure to contribute and deliver properly.
- Decide on a plan of action and clarify all follow-up steps as you conclude the meeting.
- Be mindful of tangents and keep discussions on track.

In this situation, you might feel…

Surprise

Frustration

Exasperation

Resentment

Confusion

Perplexity

Inefficiency

On est une entreprise avec des chiffres. Pas de *blabla*. C'est très structuré, très carré, centré sur l'objectif. Nos meetings sont tous comme ça. La situation, l'objectif, l'action plan. Quels chiffres il faut atteindre. C'est la notion de résultat. Sans trop penser à la connaissance des hommes. Franchement, cela manque presque d'humanité.[1]

— LOUIS, French
Health Industry, MA, U.S.

---

[1] *We're a company focused with numbers. No blah, blah, blah. It's very structured, very square, very goal oriented. Our meetings are all like that—the road map, the objective, the action plan, numbers we need to reach. It's all about results. Without caring too much about the people. Frankly, it almost lacks humanity.*

The French love meetings, especially recurring meetings. Sometimes there isn't even a real agenda or a lot to say. The intention is good—I suppose it's to bring people together—but I see no real work getting done, so it's an interesting mindset to me!

— JAIMEE, American, living in Paris
Tech. Industry, Paris, France

We, Americans, prefer to schedule meetings only if we need them. A typical meeting agenda goes like this—what is the objective of the meeting? What decisions do we need to make? *How are we going to figure it out*, etc. Versus the French enjoy heavy discussion meetings.

— TED, American
FMCG Industry, New York, U.S.

Think of a deer in a headlight. It's the symbol of the animal paralyzed when caught in the light: we don't tell the truth, because to Americans it's of no use at all. It's more about doing than criticizing.

POSITIVE SPIRIT VERSUS CRITICAL MINDSET

Pensez au symbole du *deer in a headlight*. C'est le symbole du blocage : on ne dit pas la vérité, car pour les Américains, ça ne sert à RIEN. Il faut FAIRE, plutôt que de critiquer.

— JEAN, French
   Tech. Industry, New York, U.S.

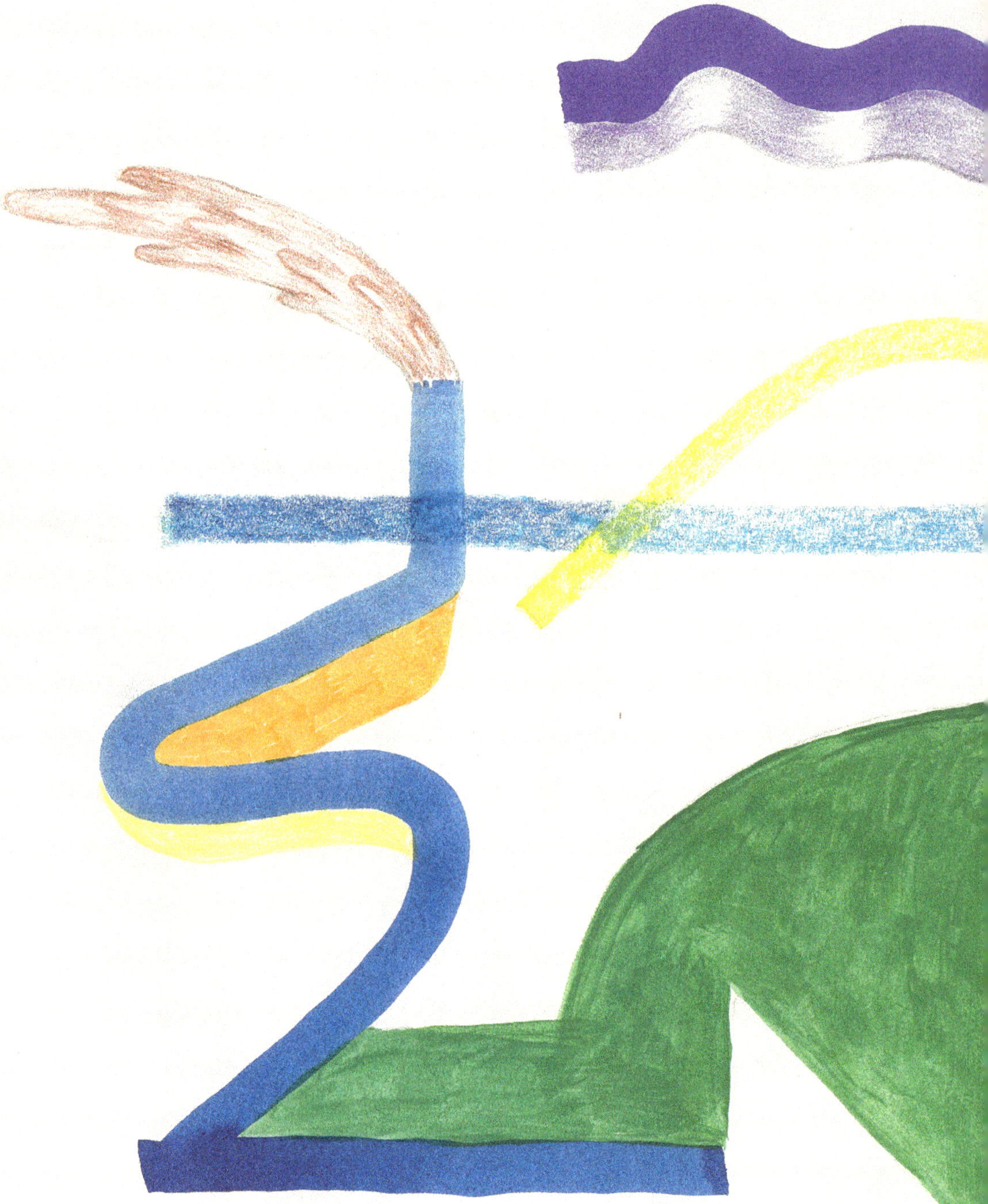

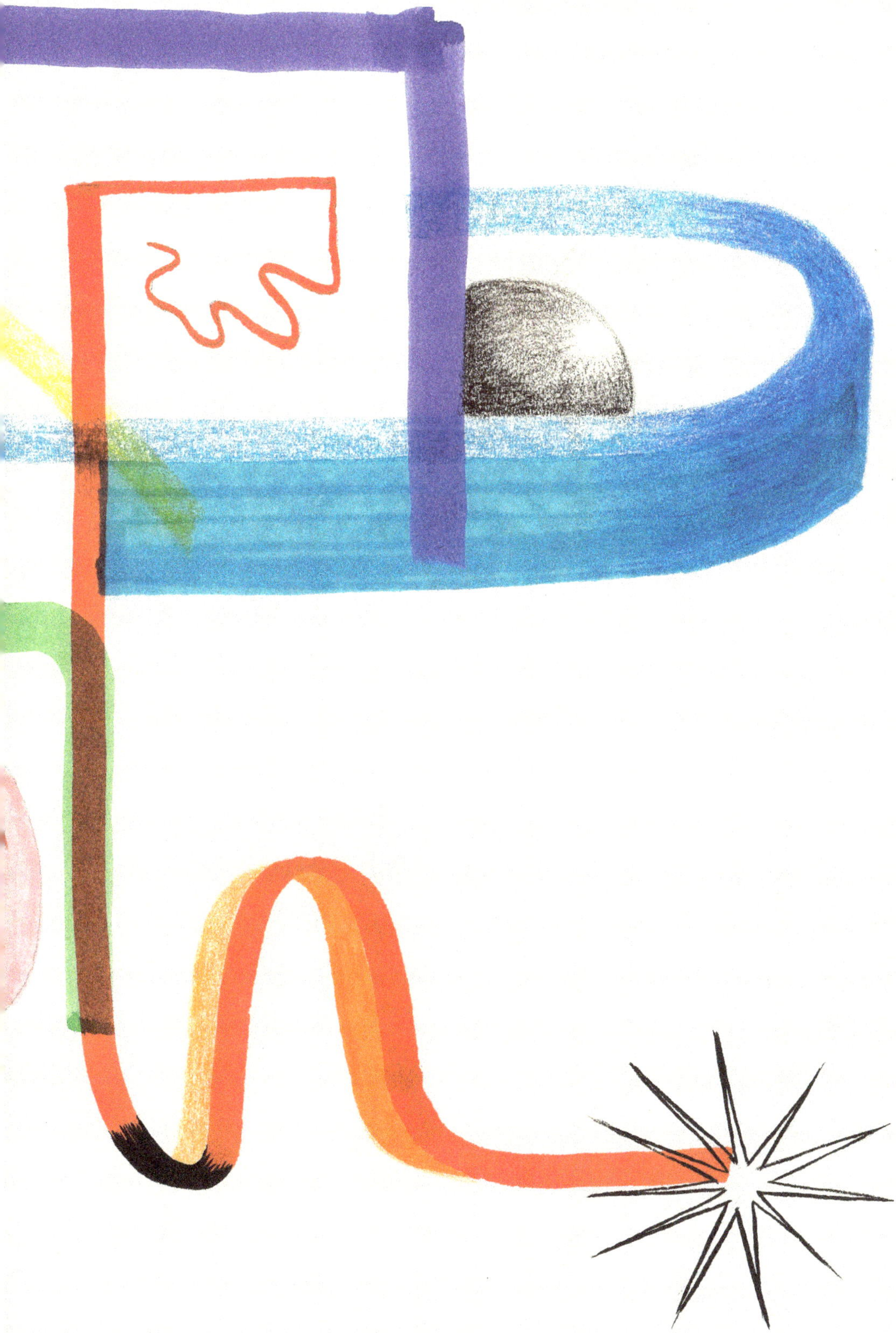

In this situation, you might feel…

Distrust

Discouragement

Judgement

Miscommunication

Irritation

Anxiety

POSITIVE and CONSENSUAL: *GET IT DONE!*

NEGATIVE and CONFLICTED: *MAKE A POINT!*

The Situation

Americans tend to be constructive and avoid conflicts in order not to hurt people's feelings. They also believe that having a positive work environment is the best way to get things done. For them, negativity is counterproductive, and may lead to a waste of time. However, this does not mean they do not have sharp opinions.

In contrast, the French enjoy openly debating and arguing in order to understand the true meaning of an idea. They are raised to express diverging or opposite views, and enjoy debating, which makes them quite often seem negative.

Tips and tricks

For Americans:
- Be aware that the French are raised to debate and express opinions vigorously.
- Don't take their remarks personally. Constructive criticism will only improve your work.
- Step back, expand on your enthusiasm… The French need to identify the situation before moving toward solutions.

For the French:
- Avoid putting people on the spot… Americans find it offensive.
- Rephrase your criticism in a constructive way to avoid hurting feelings or blockage.
- Learn to read between the lines: Americans do have an opinion, but they express it more softly.
- Think positive!

> Since HR is a safe space, people come to me all the time. I hear stories about the French making abrupt comments, having rude behavior, and interrupting people. This is really concerning as it creates a very negative atmosphere.
> — MOHAMED, Asian-American
> Retail–HR position, CA, U.S.

> We just finished a meeting and my French colleague happily came to me to say how good she felt about how it went. She didn't realize that it had actually not gone well at all. The criticism was too subtle. Therefore, I had to explain to her that Americans do not express negative comments directly, and that she needed to decode what was being said behind the words.
> — SANDRA, American
> Luxury Industry–HR position, New York, U.S.

> Si on est bloqué, parce qu'on cherche les accusations, plus personne ne fait rien. Mieux vaut être pragmatique, et ne pas chercher le responsable. En France, on a envie d'avoir raison, de montrer que l'autre a tort. Depuis que j'ai appris tout ça, je ne vais plus au clash comme avant, et ça va beaucoup mieux ![1]
> — LOUIS, French
> Health Industry, MA, U.S.

[1] *If we're stuck because we're looking for accusations, no one does anything. It's better to be pragmatic, and not look for the person at fault. In France, we want to be right, to show that the other person is wrong. Since I learned all that, I don't confront people like I used to, and it's much better!*

[2] *One cannot express one's opinion directly. What a slap in the face. When we express our opinions, we have to sugarcoat our critiques.*

On ne peut pas exprimer son opinion de manière directe. On se prend des portes. Quand on exprime nos opinions il faut *sugarcoat* nos critiques.[2]

— CONSTANCE, French
Tech. Industry, New York, U.S.

The Head of HR was telling us how devastated the American team was after a store visit from the French management team. They criticized everything and only listed the problems, overlooking Americans' achievements. We have to be aware that sometimes it creates a wall between us.

— JENNIFER, American
Food Industry, N.J.

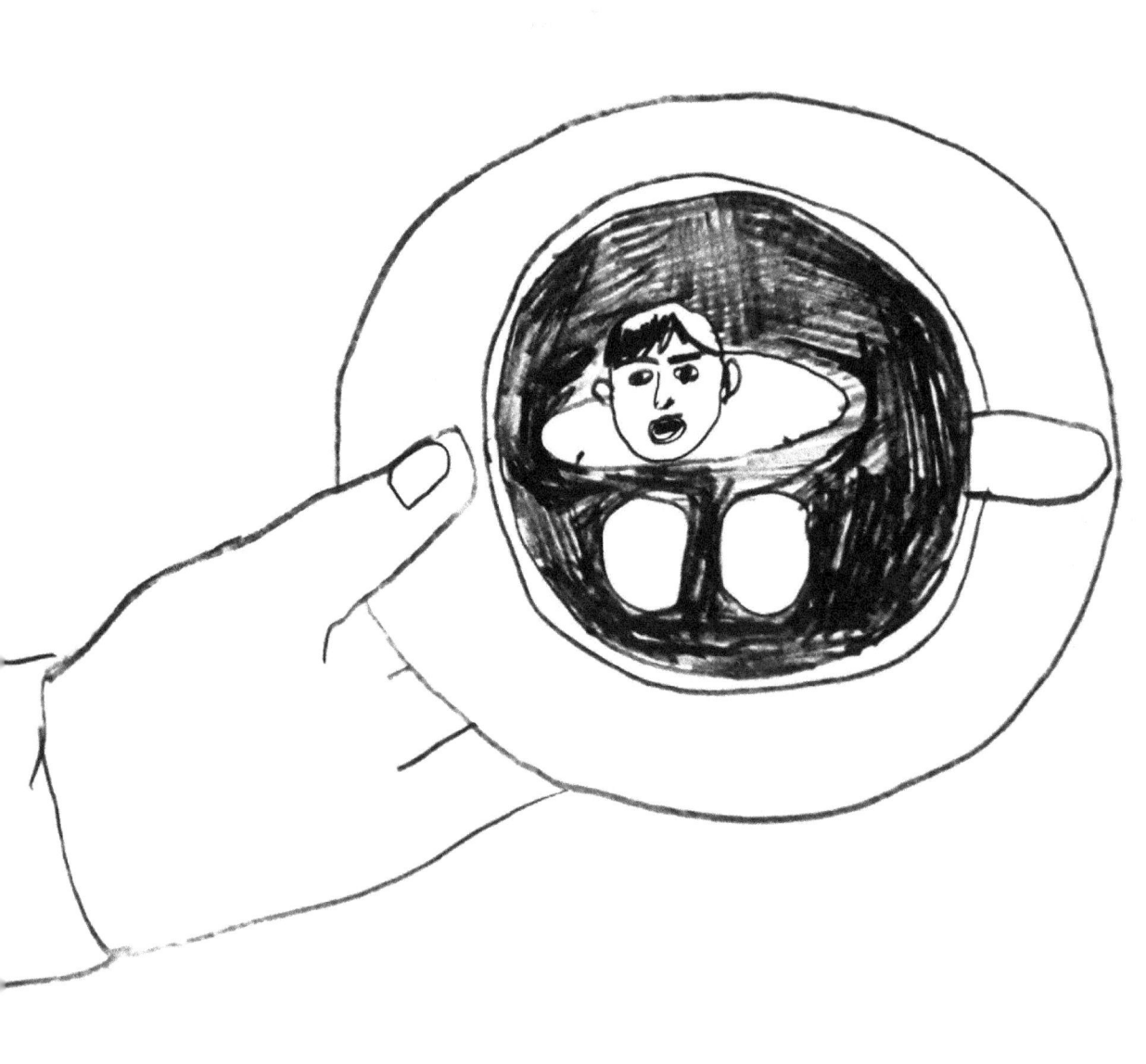

PROFESSIONAL RELATIONSHIPS

It can be nice to sit together, to take a break, and at the same time, to give space for a more personal connection, instead of Americans' *go-go-go*! But the truth is, we avoid this so we can get things done. I realize that the French always find a valuable reason to have a coffee break, in order to get to know each other. Americans never take the time for that.

— TED, American
   FMCG Industry, New York, U.S.

USEFUL RELATIONSHIPS

The Situation

Americans are used to networking. They cultivate opportunities and often demonstrate great pragmatism in relationships. These relations are explicit, reciprocal, and assumed. Their aim is not to create a friendship with their colleagues, but rather to work well together. For the French, this comes across as superficial and hypocritical. They don't understand that a transactional relationship can be just as natural and sincere.

Tips and tricks

For Americans:
- Don't get offended if the French are more reserved in the beginning; understand that they may need more time to engage.
- Enjoy meeting others without a specific purpose/agenda.
- Appreciate that the French are holistic and emotional in their relationships.

PERSONAL RELATIONSHIPS

In contrast, the French build relationships over time. They appreciate getting to know their colleagues, which may eventually lead to mixing their professional and personal lives. Americans, who are not used to this, may find this destabilizing and may interpret the French initial coldness as arrogance.

For the French:
- Be more welcoming at the beginning of a relationship, show your support, and be explicit.
- Accept and cultivate useful connections too— there's nothing wrong with pragmatism.
- Avoid judging Americans; they are not necessarily superficial!

In this situation, you might feel...

Skepticism

Disappointment

Embarrassment

Confusion

Intrusiveness

The French take more time in building relationships, but once they do, there is a very strong loyalty. In the U.S. you are less relevant, just a person. To me, the only important thing in work relationships is that we work well together.
— EMILIE, Russian-American
FMCG Industry, New York, U.S.

Les Américains adorent le *networking*. J'ai été présentée à plusieurs *events* — on te présente avec ton prénom et ton nom de famille. Les Français nous présentent rarement avec le nom de famille. Ils sont moins préparés. Alors que les Américains intègrent systématiquement cette perception que l'interlocuteur peut avoir une utilité pour plus tard, peu importe quoi.[1]
— CONSTANCE, French
Tech. Industry, New York, U.S.

Americans are very quick to engage in a conversation with others, but it takes time before they really open up. This sometimes can be frustrating or disappointing to the French.

— JACOB, American
Insurance Industry, GA, U.S.

I lived in Paris for a long time and it was great to have so many French people inviting me over to their house! But, if I have to be honest, I was afraid I would have to invite them back. Americans make a clearer separation between work and personal life.

— ROBERT, American, who spent 10 years in France
Health Industry, New Jersey, U.S.

[1] *Americans love networking. I've been introduced at several events—they introduce you with your first and last name. The French rarely introduce you with your last name. They are less prepared. Whereas Americans systematically integrate this perception that their new acquaintance can be useful for later, no matter what.*

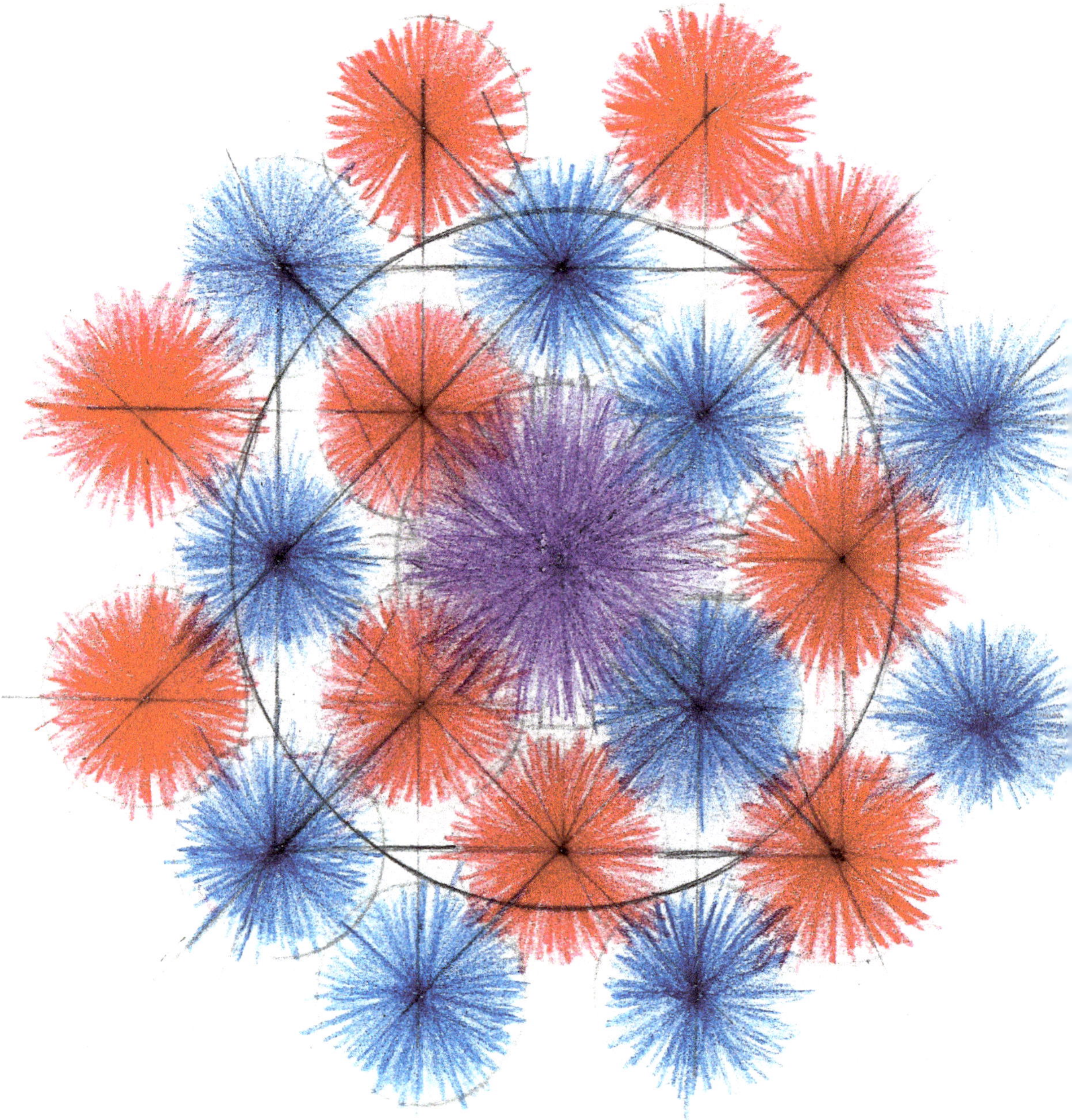

THE TEAM!
—One for all and all for one?

In France people say: *I did this*, or *I finished that*. This is different to American culture. We are all about teamwork.

— **DOROTHY, American in France
Fashion Industry Paris, France**

SHINE AS A TEAM

SHINE AS AN INDIVIDUAL

The Situation

Note: We realize, on this topic in particular, that there can be nuances from one industry to another.

Americans are experts in building teams. Everyone has a task, his/her own responsibility, but everyone is focused on the same goals. This is cultural, as they learn this from a very early age, at school and through sports.

In contrast, the French are raised to develop a singular and independent way of thinking. Their approach, or the notion of a team, comes much later when joining the corporate world, and it doesn't play out in the same way.

In some cases, this difference can result in miscommunication. Americans may put forward their result as a team, whereas the French might highlight their individual performances in priority.

Tips and tricks

For Americans:
- Encourage teamwork and collective rewards to enhance collaboration.
- Respect that the French can be more independent: give them space for their self-expression.

For the French:
- Lean in on the team.
- Let the team shine and you will shine with it.
- Engage in sport discussions: it's an integral part of team culture at work.
- Two minds think better than one: enjoy collaborations and exchanging ideas.

In this situation,
you might feel…

Mistrust

Disengagement

Demotivation

Misfit

Depreciation

Misjudgment

In the U.S., it's all about working together. Even as a junior, you are exposed to the big picture. You are aware of what the company is going for and what your boss' objectives are. In this way, you know where you fit, you feel motivated because you understand that all members of the team are part of the process, and all of them are key players to move forward.

— SANDRA, American
Luxury, New York, U.S.

Ici, les français veulent souvent briller individuellement, versus le groupe, comme ça se fait en Amérique. Cela me met toujours mal à l'aise quand je vois un Français faire ça, on est aux antipodes.[1]

— NATHALIE, French, 20 years in the U.S., FMCG Industry, IL, U.S.

I work for a French company and we don't have any team outings, like bowling or sporting events. It would be great to do some of these things to create a stronger team spirit, but I feel this is less the culture of the French people... maybe, it's also because we are a too small team here in the U.S..

— JOHN, American
Technology, New York, U.S.

Le sport pour souder les équipes, c'est hyper important pour les Américains. Ils en parlent car c'est un sujet qui symbolise l'excellence du groupe. Je l'ai compris en étudiant le football américain — *the success* — c'est qu'il y a une place pour tout le monde. Le gros à l'avant, le petit derrière qui va vite et les *pompom girls*... Tout ça, c'est le groupe qui dépasse les excellences individuelles. Nous, les Français, on n'y arrivera pas tant qu'on ne comprendra pas cela.[2]

— THOMAS, French
Tech. Industry, New York, U.S.

[1] *Here, the French often want to shine individually, versus the group, as it works in America. It always makes me uncomfortable when I see a French guy doing that, we are the opposite.*

[2] *The sport of team bonding is very important to Americans. They talk about it because it's a subject that symbolizes the excellence of the group. I understood it when I got into American football—success is that there is a place for everyone. The big guy in front, the little guy in the back who goes fast, and the cheerleaders. It's all about the group exceeding individual excellence. We, the French, won't get there until we understand that.*

I had a lecture on good and great as part of a new marketing plan for one of our brands. Well, during this session, I learned that good is not good, that great has become the new good. Here you never know where to stand. In a meeting, if someone says good to me ... I'm not sure if it's good. You really have to decode it.

THE MEANINGS BEHIND THE WORDS

J'ai eu un cours sur le *Good and Great*, dans le cadre d'un nouveau plan Marketing pour l'une de nos marques. Et bien, pendant cette session, j'ai appris que *good* c'est pas bien, que *great* est devenu le nouveau *good*. Ici on ne sait jamais sur quel pied danser ! En réunion si on me dit *good* … je ne suis pas sûr que ce soit bon. Il faut vraiment décoder.

— MARC, French
  Luxury Industry, New York, U.S.

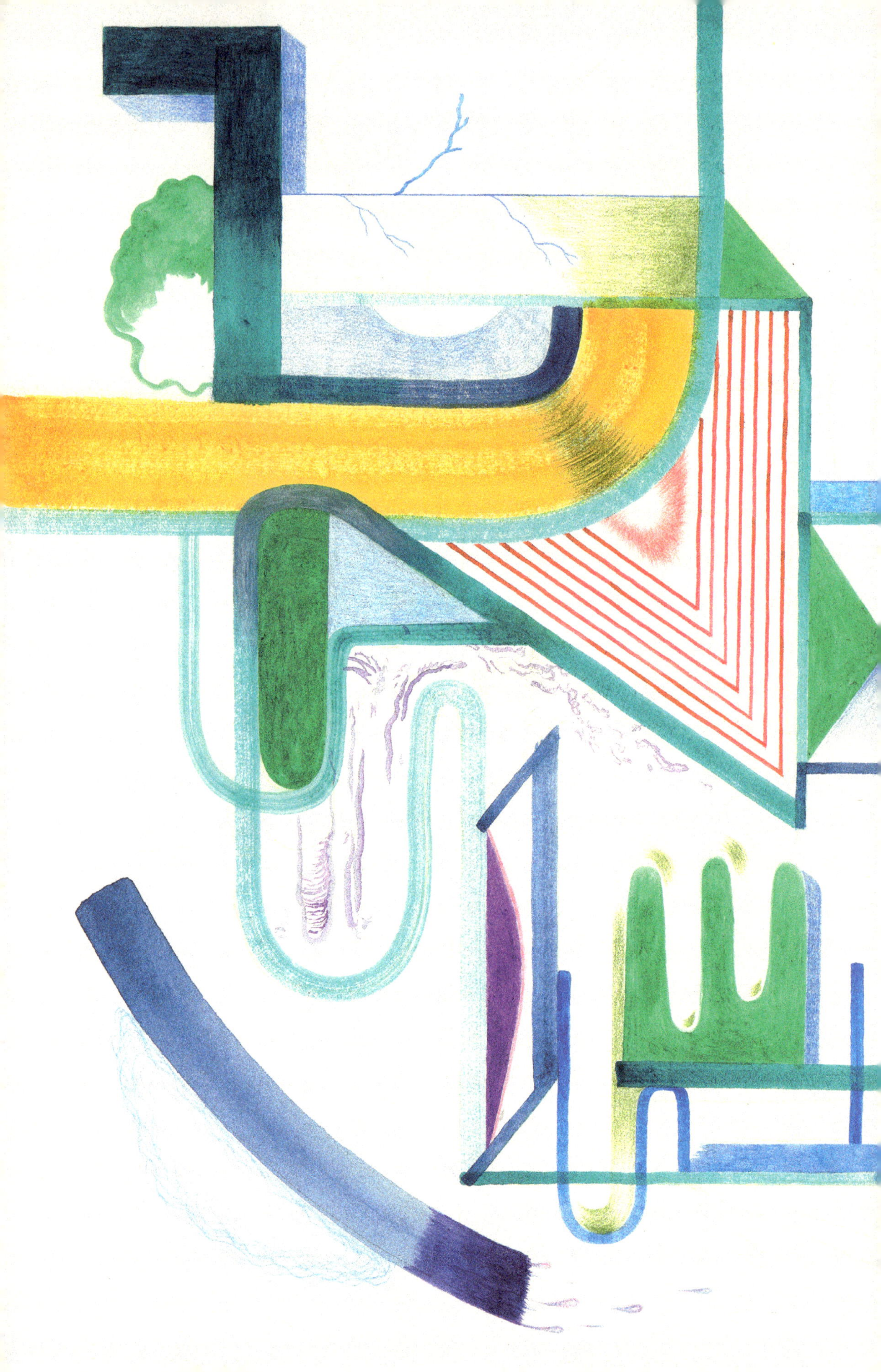

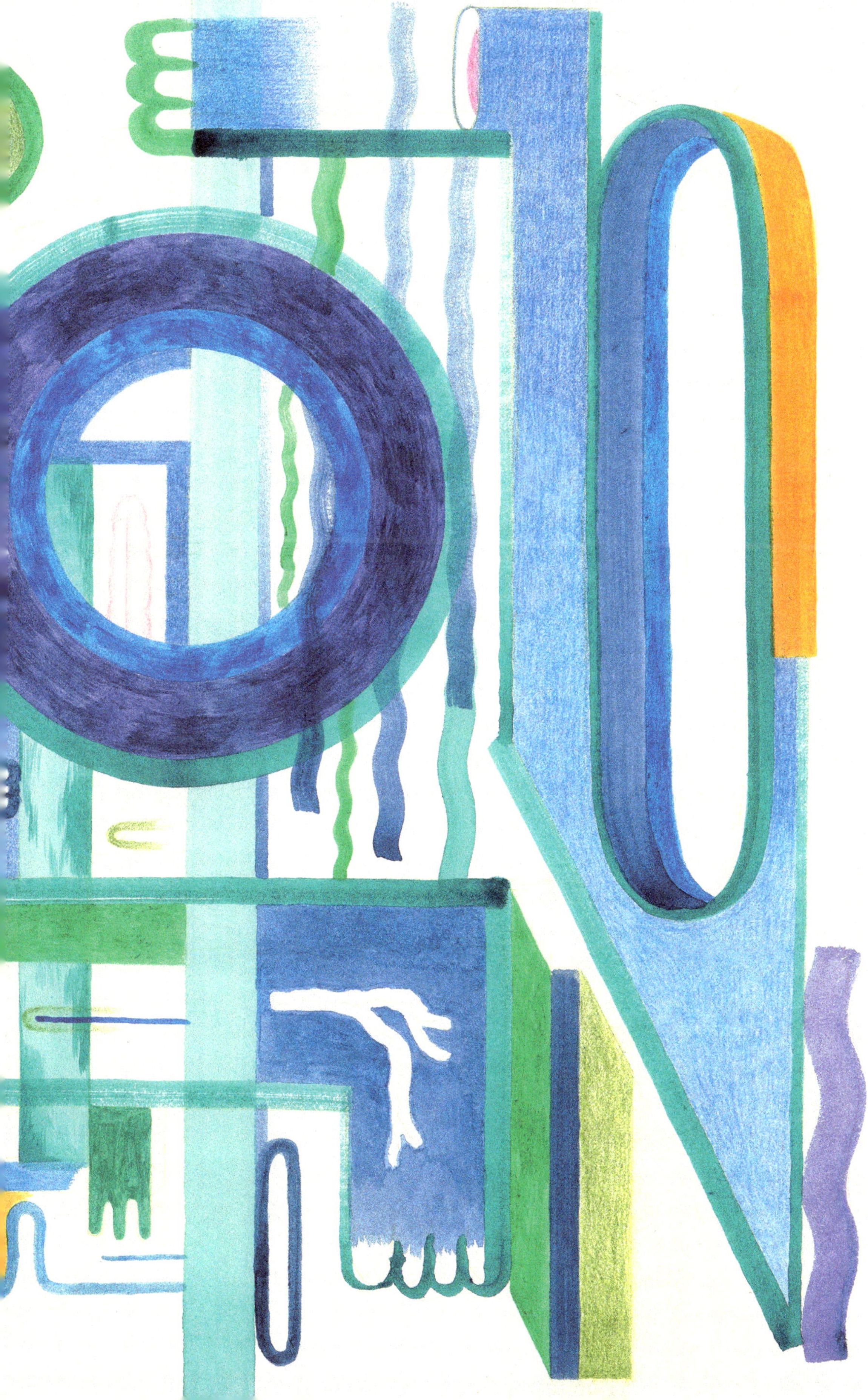

THE GREAT   THE GOOD

The Situation

Americans are likely to overemphasize and be incredibly encouraging to make people feel good about their work. Their criticism can be cryptic and not explicit for the French. To the French, however, this may come across as exaggerated and even misleading; they don't understand the nuances behind the words used by Americans.

In contrast, the French, having an opinion about pretty much everything, are very vocal on it, and in a straightforward manner. It is not personal. They just don't feel a need to sugarcoat what they are trying to say. However, this can be offensive to Americans and perceived as rude.

Such difference in the semantics is obvious during the evaluation process, but it goes much beyond: it affects all type of professional interactions, with colleagues, clients and suppliers too.

Tips and Tricks

For Americans:
- When you use superlatives, try to explain why and provide concrete examples to support your comment.
- Dare to be more explicit in your observations/discussions.
- Understand the French do not realize the impact of their words, as they are used to being more direct and less positive.

For the French:
- Be mindful about the impact of the words you use.
- Inquire more about the meaning of words (e.g., dig in: What is good/great about it? What are the specific needs?).
- Go beyond! You know Americans like to use superlatives.

In this situation, you might feel...

Skepticism

Frustration

Misunderstanding

Confusion

Misjudgment

We have a tendency to sugarcoat everything. For instance, when I write down a negative comment, I always put a smiley face next to it, so it seems less harsh. We also like to say *it's great, it's amazing*, and then change everything if the result is not that great. This is how we are. We just can't help it.

— SAMANTHA, American
Luxury Industry, New York, U.S.

Nous avions un chef de produit Américain qui nous a dit combien il était excité par le nouveau produit qu'on allait lancer, convaincu qu'il allait *transformer le marché* et *faire croître l'entreprise de façon exponentielle*. Notre ingénieur français et moi-même avons pensé que le gars marchait au crack en l'écoutant, tellement c'était exagéré.[1]

— DIDIER, French
Tech. Industry, New York, U.S.

En Amérique, c'est le *beyond amazing*! Le côté ultra positif dans la forme des Américains. Leur côté *Amazing, Incroyable, Awesome*, c'est standard. On pourrait écrire plusieurs pages là-dessus. En fait ils pensent que c'est de la merde et tu ne le sauras pas.[2]

— CLÉMENT, French
Spirits Industry, New York, U.S.

In France, strong negative words are not a real issue, whereas in English their meaning can be truly distressing. For example, I asked a French colleague for her opinion on something, I think it was about my new suit, and she said, *Oh, c'est moche!* without realizing that this really hurt me. The French don't realize the impact of what they say.

— SARAH, American
Finance, New York, U.S.

Le français critique, mais en fait ça l'intéresse, alors que l'Américain ne dit pas ce qu'il pense de manière explicite. Donc il faut décrypter le vrai sens des mots. C'est très frappant, en particulier quand tu pitch pour un appel d'offres. Tu y vas, tu déroules ton histoire, tu penses qu'ils adorent ton idée, mais en fait s'ils n'en veulent pas ou s'ils ne veulent pas faire de business avec toi ils ne te le disent pas. Du coup, tu perds le client mais tu ne sais pas vraiment pourquoi ! Ça m'est arrivé plusieurs fois.[3]

—THOMAS, French
Entrepreneur, New York, U.S.

---

[1] *We had an American product manager who told us how excited he was about the new product we were going to launch, absolutely convinced that it would transform the market and grow the business exponentially. Our French engineer and I thought the guy was on drugs as we listened to him, it was so over the top.*

[2] *In the U.S. everything is the beyond amazing! The ultra-positive side in the style of the Americans. Their amazing, incredible, awesome, it's standard. We could write several pages about it. They actually think it's junk and you won't know it.*

[3] *The French person criticizes, but he's actually interested, whereas the American doesn't say what he thinks explicitly. We have to decipher the true meaning of the words. It's very striking, especially when you're pitching a deal. You go for it, you tell your story, you think they love your idea, but at the end, if they don't want it, nor want to do business with you, they don't tell you either way. Ultimately, you lose the client, but you don't really know why! It's happened to me several times.*

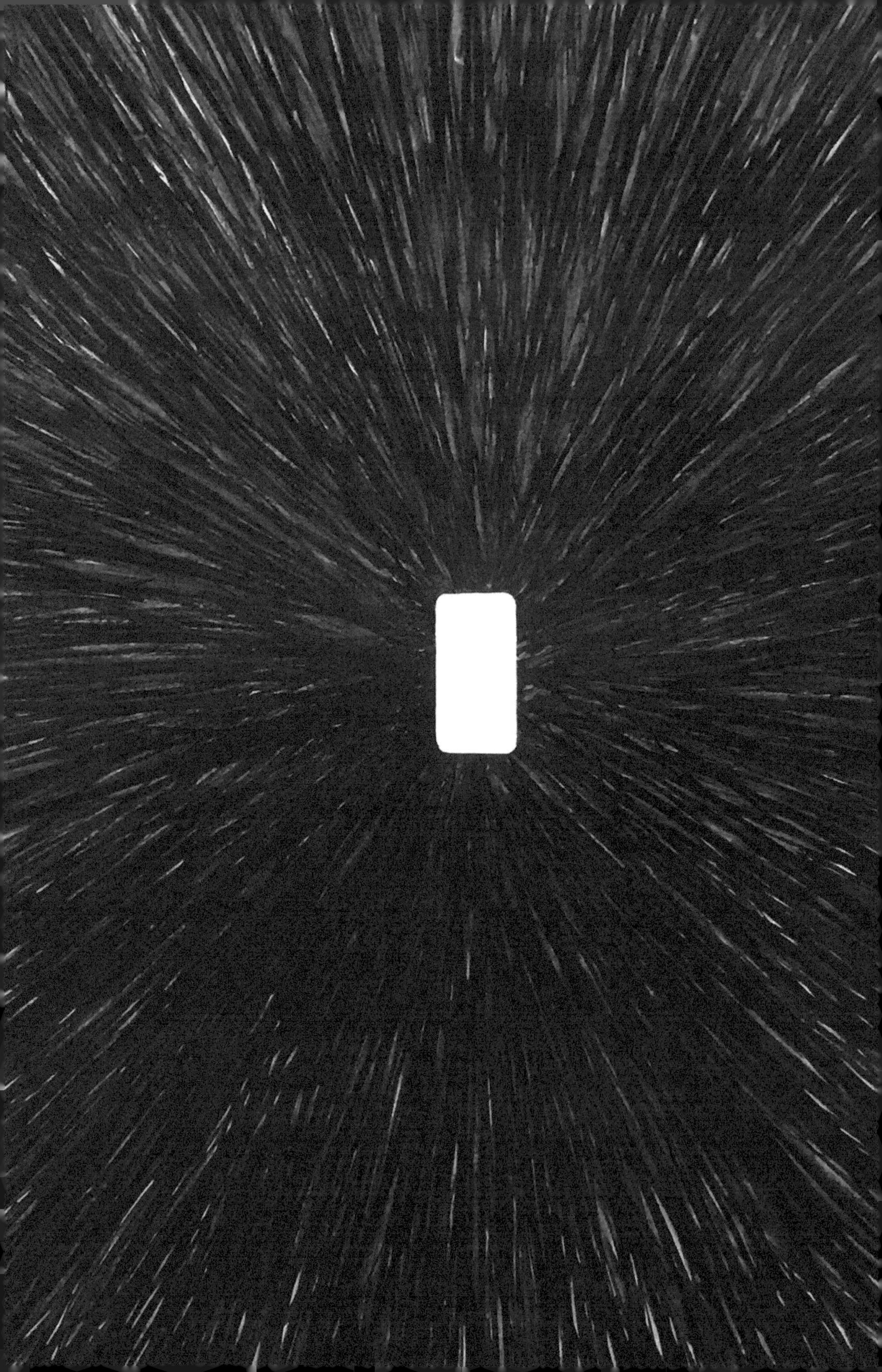

DID YOU SAY EXPERTISE?

Je recherchais un comptable. Je trouve une comptable américaine, et bien vous savez quoi ? Elle fait, soit la compta fournisseur, soit la compta client! Donc ici c'est le silo. L'hyper-spécialisation. Ça rend les choses très compliquées.

— CLAIRE, French, 10 years in the U.S
Luxury Industry, New York, U.S.

I was looking for an accountant. I found an American accountant. Well, you know what? She's either an accounts payable specialist or accounts receivable specialist. This is a silo situation. A hyper-specialization mode. It makes things very complicated.

In this situation, you might feel…

Distrust
Frustration
Vulnerability
Isolation
Dissatisfaction
Misalignment

SPECIALISTS   GENERALISTS

The Situation

Culturally, in the U.S., each person specializes based on their strengths. They are used to bringing their specific competencies to the team. Job descriptions and work assignments are more targeted. For Americans, their focus is the team, and they want to contribute by bringing what they are strongest at.

In contrast, the French working mode is different. People are trained to have a holistic view on things. They approach work and business with a broader perspective, even if they are also very detail-oriented. It is not unusual to broaden work assignments and go beyond narrow job descriptions.

These differences make recruiting difficult for both parties. When the French want to hire an American talent, there is a lot of frustration, as it gets more difficult to find someone who can accomplish multiple tasks. Americans who are looking for true specialists, experts in their own field, may think that the French employee is a *jack-of-all-trades, master of none*.

Tips and tricks

For Americans:
- Be open to expanding your professional horizons, even in areas that aren't your forte! It's a great way to improve your skills, explore your potential, and boost your value as a professional.
- Be curious about the work your colleagues are assigned to.
- Learn to think holistically.

For the French:
- Create opportunities for ownership to help Americans take charge: They are capable of substantial contributions when allowed to plan and share a more comprehensive perspective.
- Learn to delegate and to trust: It will increase your efficacy and amplify your achievements.
- Identify your specific technical expertise.

C'est une question de culture. En Amérique, par exemple, tu as cela au resto—c'est fragmenté, il y a une personne différente pour chaque tâche. En France, tu as un serveur et il s'occupe de tout. Ici c'est le spécialisme à outrance.[1]

— PIERRE, French
Finance, IL, U.S.

The French are taught to be well-rounded and have a general sense of business. It must come from the way they're educated. In France, you have access to a world-class education for far less money than in the U.S. It definitely causes envy. On the other hand, Americans are experts in their field, which is attractive in its own way.

— ROBERT, lived 10 years in France
Health Industry, MA, U.S.

> In the U.S., it's more about expertise. You pick a direction and you go for it. Americans are usually brought in for specific skills.
> — ADAM, American
> Finance, New York, U.S.

> En France on peut gérer, depuis la créa jusqu'au coding. En Amérique, on ne peut pas. Ou tu dessines, ou tu codes ! C'est hyper frustrant.[2]
> — DIDIER, French
> Tech. Industry
> New York, U.S.

[1] *It's all about culture. For instance, In America, you have this in restaurants—it's a fragmented workforce. There's a different person for each task. In France, you have just one waiter and he take care of everything. Here it's all about over-specialization.*

[2] *In France we can manage everything, the creation and the coding. In America, we can't. Either you draw or you code! It's very frustrating.*

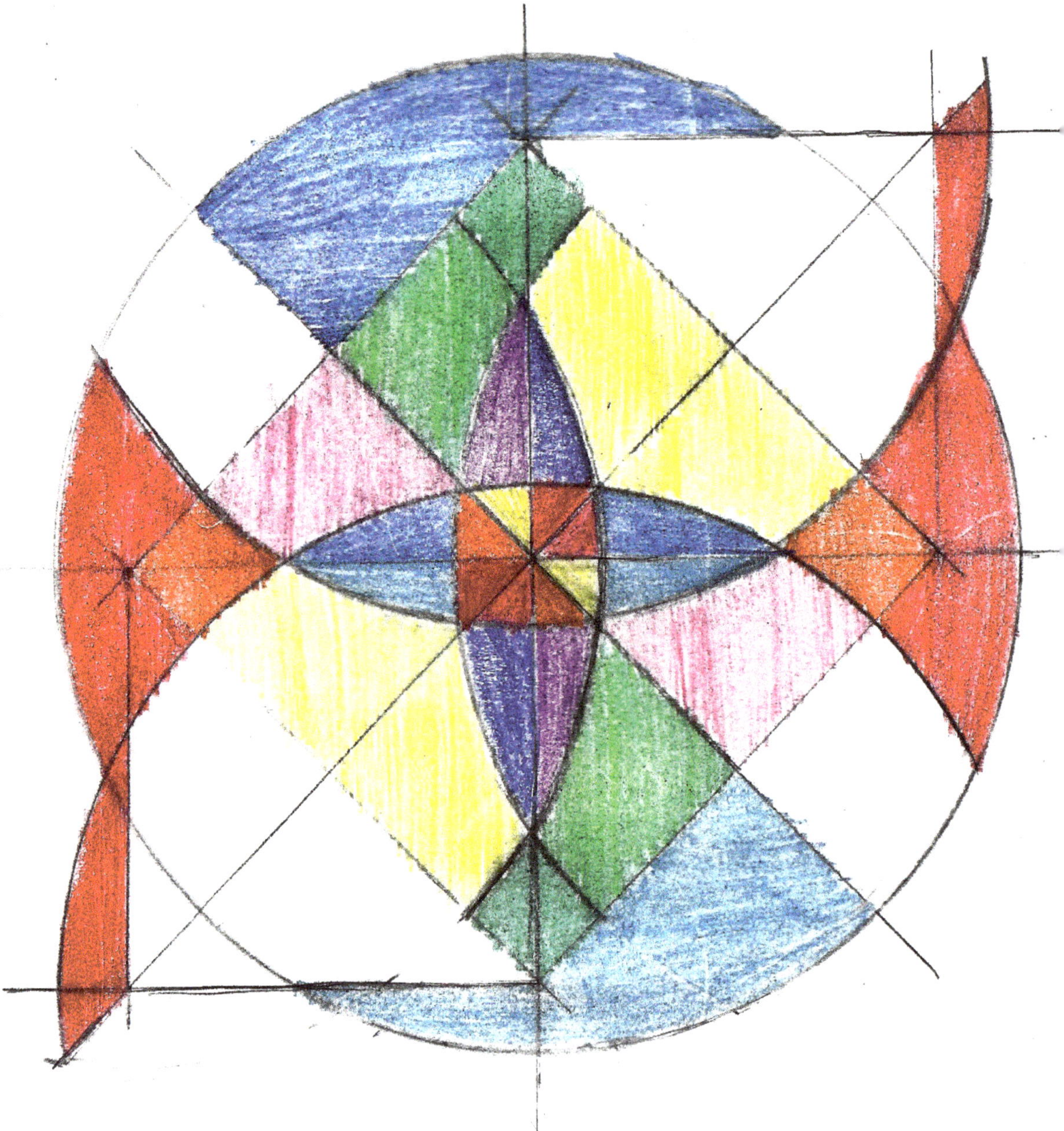

WORK STYLES AND SOCIAL CODES OF CONDUCT

Our boss is French, and still comes up to each of us, every morning, to shake hands. I am an easygoing person, so it's ok, but at the same time, I'm a germaphobe. Every time, I go and wash my hands afterwards, or use my sanitizer generously! We laugh about it. I think it is very courteous, but still, he continues to do so. But it's fine. I have to admit it's a bit uncomfortable for me.

— JOHN, American
   Tech. Industry, New York, U.S.

CASUAL AND WELCOMING

FORMAL AND CODED

The Situation

Americans have a friendly style and seem relaxed in the office. They favor collaboration and derive value from strong team dynamics where every member contributes in a way that seems quite informal. Their pragmatic nature might perceive formalities as stuffy and counterintuitive, in contrast to their more spontaneous office culture. For the French this may seem too friendly and acts like giving hugs (although they give kisses!), are private affairs.

In contrast, given their education, the French have a hard time dropping the formalities, which are how they demonstrate respect and show manners. The overtly casual nature of Americans can make them feel very uncomfortable. These cultural differences can read as cold and be taken personally by Americans who are already put off by the prevalence of so many formalities.

Tips and Tricks

For Americans:
- Understand that France has a culture of strictly enforced social codes.
- Don't take it personally! If the French do not respond with the enthusiasm you expected, it's not about you.
- Give the French time to acclimate to your vastly different system, they will impress you with their loyalty over time.

For the French:
- Embrace spontaneity!
- Adopt some of their camaraderie. It's the best way to create team bonds!
- Accept the Americans' more casual outlook and approach. Know that it is sincere: They have a generous spirit and like to show they care.

In this situation, you might feel...

Discomfort

Embarrassment

Awkwardness

Rigidity

Disrespect

The fact that you don't have to worry about using the formal *vous* or informal *tu* and we all use first names—that is really cool. No artificial values, just straight casualness. The American easily says, *Oh you look cute… oh this… oh that…* It's just about being nice to each other! It feels good.

— NATHALIE, French, 20 years in the USA
FMCG Industry, GA, U.S

On voit le sourire derrière le téléphone. Ils sont contents de venir bosser et généralement très accueillants. En France c'est bien plus froid, distant et formel.[1]

— JOHN, American
Tech. Industry, New York, U.S.

On te dit tout le temps *You look great, I love your shoes…* Qui que tu croises, il y aura toujours un compliment — ce qui signifie que ton interlocuteur t'a regardé ! Au début je ne savais pas quoi dire. On est à la frontière de l'hypocrisie et de la gentillesse. Si on lit cela avec notre esprit de Français — ça serait autre chose, *this is really that I care about you — tu n'es pas transparente*.[2]

— MARIE, French
Fashion Industry, New York, U.S.

---

[1] *You can see the smile behind the phone. They are happy to come to work and generally very welcoming. In France it's much colder, more distant and formal.*

[2] *You look great… I love your shoes… Whoever you meet, there is always a compliment, which means that the person you're talking to has looked at you! The first time, I didn't know what to say! We're on the borderline between hypocrisy and kindness. If we read this with our French mind: I care about you, you are not transparent.*

The French team was visiting our N.Y. office, and I thought it would be a good opportunity for them to meet the entire team, so I wanted to put together a welcome breakfast. The French team didn't want to have the entire team there, though, and preferred a smaller, more selective group. I felt humiliated because my *American-style* welcome was ignored, and my effort to integrate was denigrated. I saw this as a French-style operation, just like at home…
— LAURA, American, lived in France
Spirits Industry, New York, U.S.

Les *thank you cards*…Alala! Pour moi c'est un cauchemar, je n'y arrive pas ! Quand des gens quittent l'équipe, en fin d'année…ils nous donnent à tous des cartes. Ça fait vraiment plaisir. C'est comme pour Thanksgiving — c'est l'expression de sa gratitude — mais nous les Français on n'a tellement pas l'habitude de ces grosses démonstrations collectives.[3]
— DELPHINE, French
Beauty Industry, IL, U.S.

[3] *The thank you cards… My Goodness! For me it's a nightmare—I can't do it! When people leave the team or it's the end of the year, we always get cards. It's really nice. The same for Thanksgiving—it's an expression of gratitude. But we, French people, are so unused to these big collective courtesy demonstrations.*

GIVE FEEDBACK
—But how?

The French are more conservative when it comes to feedback and reviews. At best, they put *meets expectations* versus Americans who put *exceeds expectations* everywhere. We must therefore try not to take things personally when dealing with the French.

— ADAM, English American
　Finance, New York, U.S.

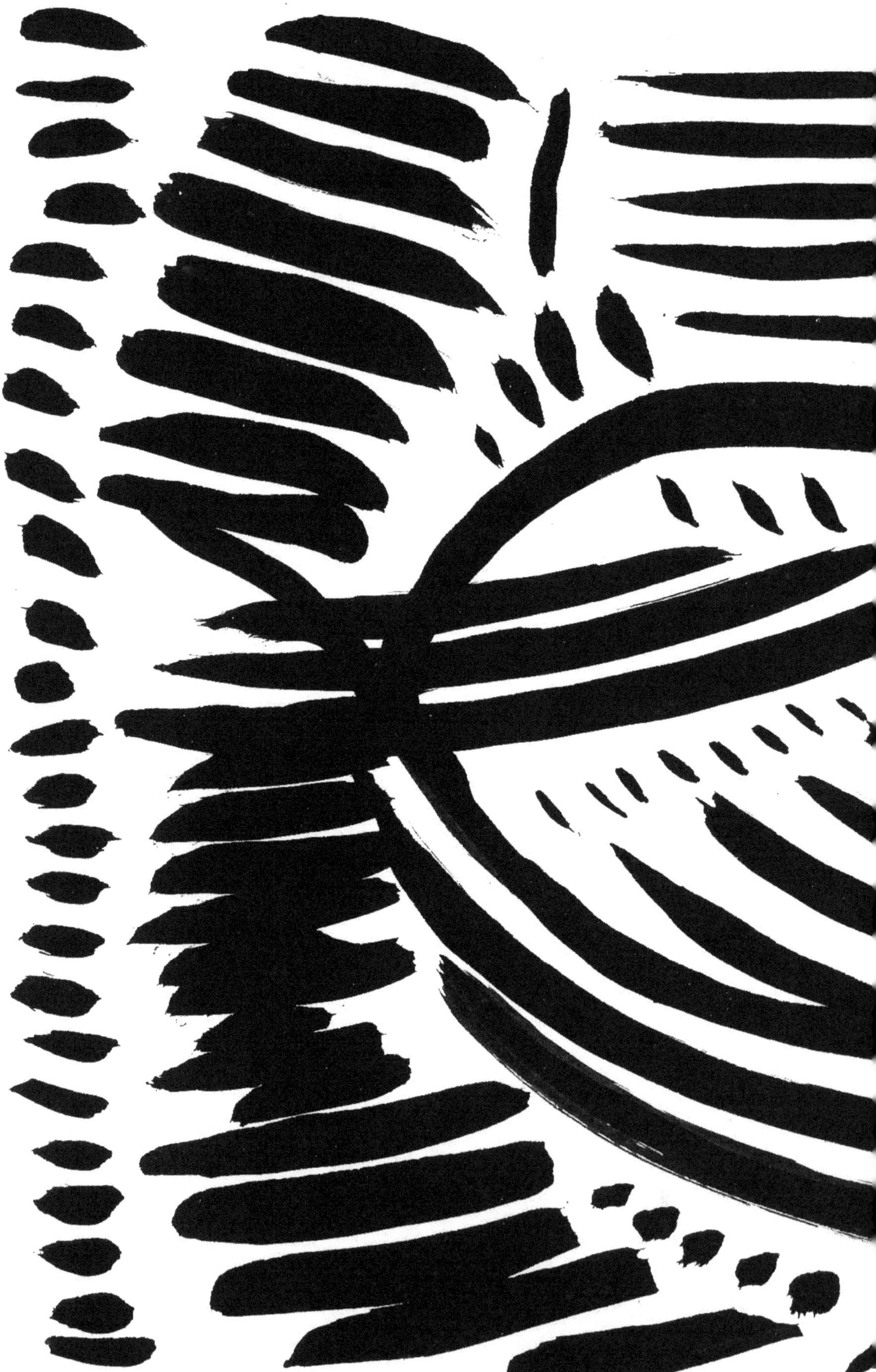

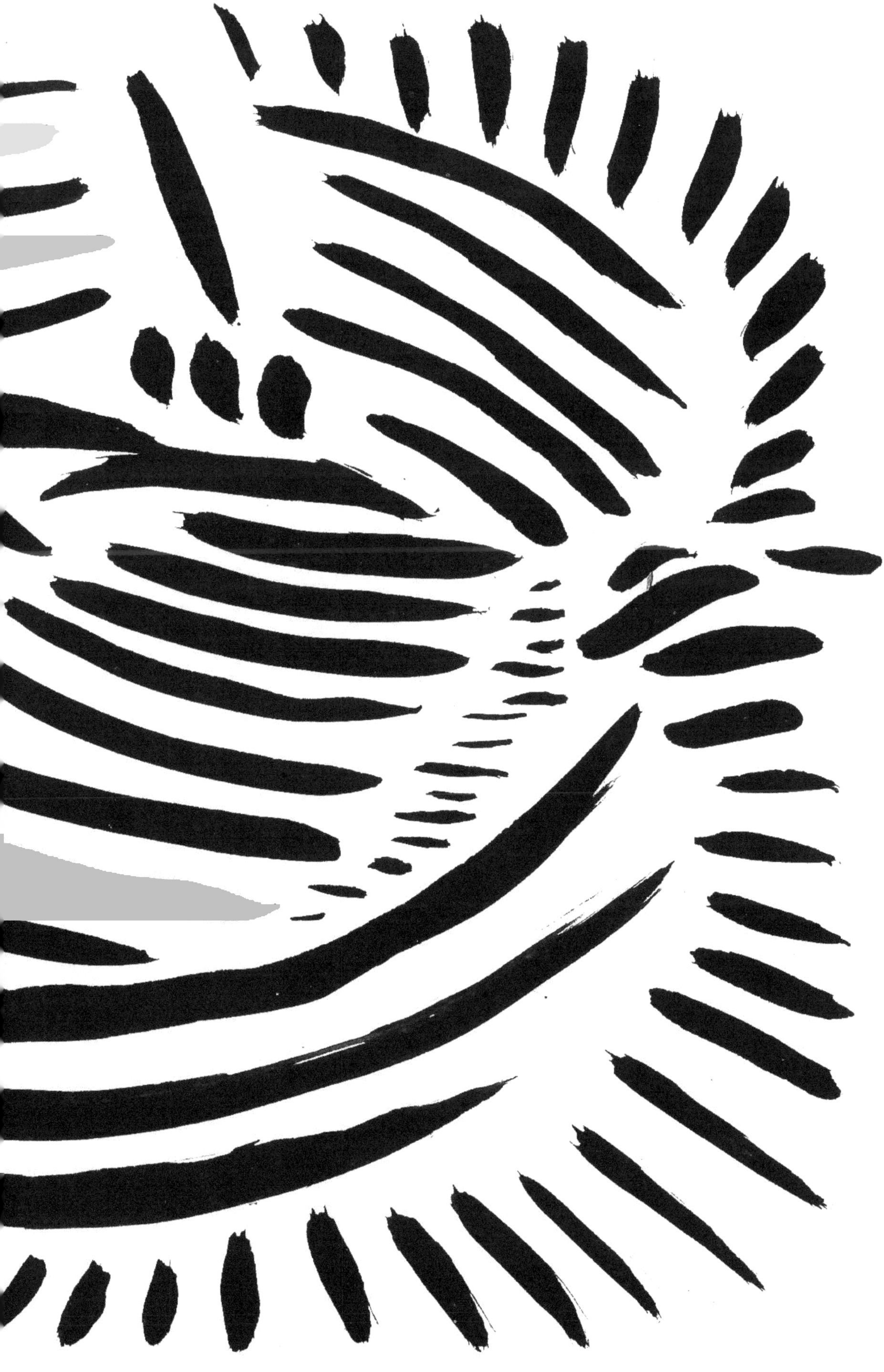

In this situation, you might feel…

Vulnerability

Surprise

Demotivation

Shame

Mistrust

Confusions

REALISTIC AT THE EXPENSE OF HURTING

POSITIVE AT THE EXPENSE OF BLURRING WHAT SUCCESS MEANS

The Situation

Many French move to the U.S. for management positions. When the performance review season starts, they receive the self-assessment forms from their subordinates and/or teams. This is a real moment of truth! While they might be expecting a mix of grades including lower ones, with some notes on what did not go well, they discover only high grades and amazing achievements! When the discussion happens, the gap between the two perceptions makes the resolution truly difficult to find, and quickly becomes a dead end. The French boss feels at risk of losing his/her authenticity by accepting feedback that does not seem accurate.

For an American, reporting to a French boss can be a real issue: Such directness can block communication, generating a loss of motivation, and even humiliation. The reverse situation is as difficult: French subordinates might struggle to obtain the recognition they deserve as compared with their American colleagues, just because their self-evaluation will be less positive than the usual American standards. They might miss opportunities to get promoted and grow as fast and get truly confused about their actual performance.

Basically, for some, pointing out the mistakes is the way to discuss improvements when for the others, the focus is always on opportunities to improve. And grades follow this logic. Such discrepancy can be difficult to handle on a global level. It is important to make sure there is harmonization and discussion.

Tips and tricks

For the French:
- Learn and respect the differences in the rating system.
- Review your team assessment with someone who knows the American grading standards before sharing.
- Avoid direct feedback that can seem too harsh.
- Always start with positive feedback.
- Instead of focusing on problems, turn the feedback into improvement opportunities.

For Americans:
- Know that French education is centered around critics. People are not used to compliments or encouragements, which seems unauthentic if excessive.
- Be mindful, the French rating is different, meaning that any negative feedback should not be taken too personally.
- Try to be as honest as possible while recognizing your own areas of improvement.

Americans are gentler while doing the review than the French. People need positive feedback. You can still be honest but say things in a nice way. The French are so direct and dry! It is really hard and pretty discouraging.

— SARAH, American
Finance, New York, U.S.

J'étais très cassant — je disais : *c'est de la merde*. Moi j'étais comme cela. Ici cela ne passe pas, ce n'est pas accepté. Donc j'essaie de faire attention. Je sais que je vais faire un reproche mais je cherche toujours le positif pour contrebalancer. Et maintenant, on upgrade tout le monde. On met des A+ et des B+ partout. Au final, c'est super positif et on fait mieux passer les messages — c'est devenu des techniques de management — Mais moi, j'ai eu du mal à apprendre tout ça.[1]

— NADINE, French
Finance, New York, U.S.

I have a background in HR, therefore a French friend of mine asked me to help her to frame some performance reviews. We cleaned up the negative wording and she was able to share the feedback much more smoothly with her team.

— HELEN, American
Hospitality, London, U.K.

Americans are very sensitive. We take things very personally. The frankness is harder on us. We are not used to hearing this so directly.

— DOROTHY, American living in France
Fashion Industry, Paris, France

> Ma HR me dit tout le temps qu'en tant que boss, je dois apprendre à faire du positive renforcement. Au début je trouvais cela vraiment pas naturel. En fait c'est bien de commencer par le positif, c'est tellement plus agréable !²

— NADINE, French
Finance, New York, U.S.

> La première année, la période des entretiens était le délire total ! Je n'avais que des auto-évals parfaites, de toute mon équipe. *Always beyond amazing.* J'étais vachement emmerdé. Nous en France, on regarde le négatif avant le positif. Du coup pour moi, le point c'était de prouver à chacun qu'il n'était pas *amazing*. Cela tournait au négatif et cela les a tous braqués, ils n'étaient plus motivés. Donc, maintenant je pousse pour du *fair*, cela me permet de me sentir plus authentique.³

— MARC, French
Luxury Industry, New-York, U.S.

---

¹ *I was very rigid—I said* This is junk. *I was like that. Here, it neither passes nor is accepted. I try to be careful. I know I'm going to make a criticism, but I'm always looking for the positive to counterbalance it. And now, we motivate everyone. We're putting A+ and B+ everywhere. At the end of the day, it's super positive and we get the message across far better. That became a management technique—but I had a hard time learning that.*

² *My HR manager is always telling me that as a boss, I have to learn how to do positive reinforcement. At first, I found it really unnatural. Actually, it's good to start with the positive, it's so much more enjoyable!*

³ *The first year, the annual reviews period was total delirium! I got only perfect self-evaluations from my entire team. Always beyond amazing. I was in a tough spot. In France, we look at the negative before the positive, which means for me, the point was to prove to everyone that they weren't amazing. But then everything turned to the negative and that upset everyone; none of the team was motivated anymore. Now I go for* fair *and it makes me feel more authentic.*

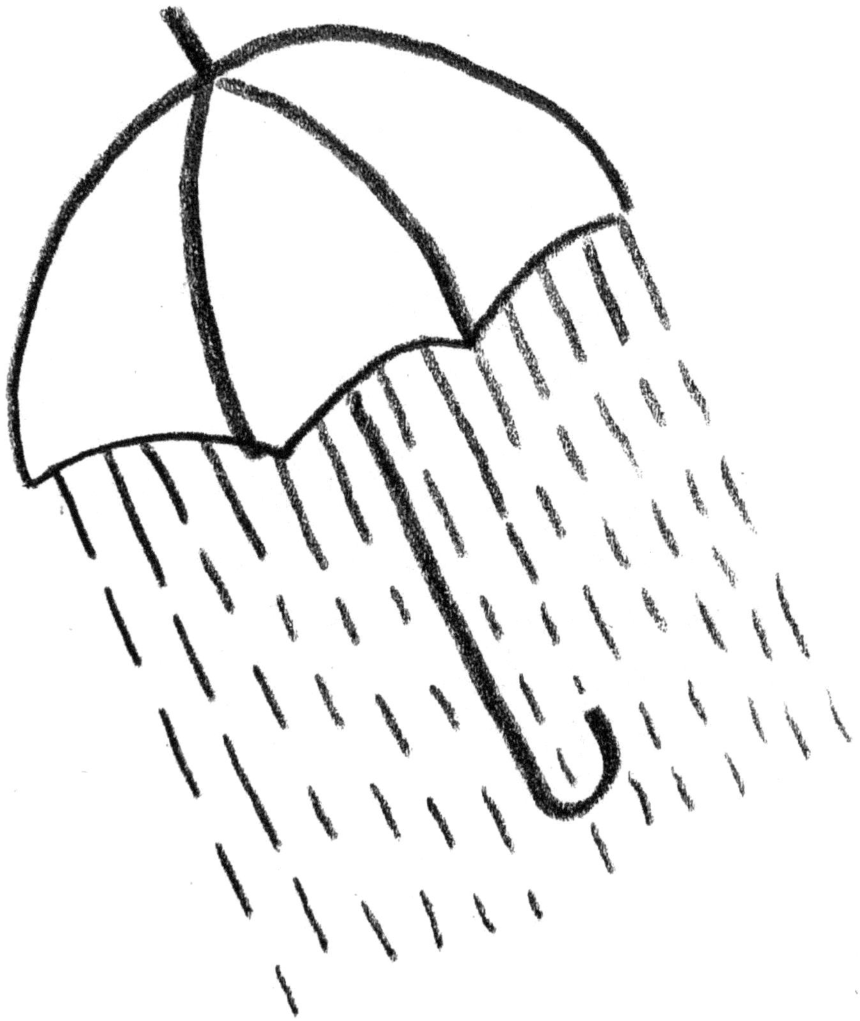

THE DO'S AND DON'TS
— THE TABOOS

Je considère toujours que si je parle en public, c'est comme si quelqu'un m'enregistrait. Cela veut dire que je fais tout le temps très attention à ce que je dis. Pour moi, c'est très dur et très déstabilisant. Il n'y a pas d'humour, il ne faut pas vexer les gens. Donc on est comme des robots — *I feel I am no longer a human being!*

— **NICOLAS, French**
  Spirits Industry, New York, U.S.

I always consider that if I speak in public, it is as if someone is recording me. That means I'm always very careful about what I say. For me, it's very hard and very unsettling. There's no humor, you can't offend people. We are kind of robots—I feel I am no longer a human being!

In this situation,
you might feel…

Fear

Anxiety

Discomfort

Apprehension

Sadness

Confusion

Stress

POLITICAL CORRECTNESS

PROVOCATION YET RESERVE

The Situation

Despite their relatively casual demeanors, Americans are stringent about what is appropriate to say or to talk about in the office. Topics like, politics, religion, race, gender, and sex are taboo, and there are rules of conduct enforced by Human Resources to ensure no one feels disrespected, hurt, or offended. Considering the level of diversity in the U.S. this all makes sense.

In contrast, the French like to speak freely and enjoy being provocative, preferring to interact with their colleagues as people, not just as co-workers. They like to make jokes and also like to speak up about their opinions. Politics, religion, race, gender, and sex, everything comes up with no restrictions. In contrast, unlike the Americans, they are not comfortable talking about money which they consider a private matter.

Obviously, this causes tensions between the two parties. On certain topics, Americans think the French can be intrusive or inappropriate, and often, French humor falls flat for this reason. The French find Americans overly sensitive and find their rules stifling: especially considering the legal ramifications over harassment claims. For the French, such conservative rules make them feel stifled and like they have to hide their personalities. But when it comes to other topics such as money (salaries, bonus…), the perception shifts.

Tips and tricks

For Americains:
- Train the French immediately and explain what is acceptable and what is not. There might be bumps along the road, but communication is key.
- Be patient.
- While it is fair to expect a particular type of professionalism, also understand that the French likely meant no offense!

For the French:
- Learn the rules and respect them.
- Participate and ask for training.
- Soften your behavior and also your language.
- Understand that Americans simply don't broach the same topics as the French and adapt your jokes.

The French make provocative jokes! This is really interesting to me, and the more French people I meet, the more I get it. It's a big difference since, in the American culture, there is no talk of politics, religion, or sex—these are all big don'ts!

—MOHAMED, Asian-American
Retail, CA, U.S.

J'arrive dans les bureaux, je vois une assistante de direction, ravissante. Je la regarde deux minutes. Le boss me voit. Il est mort de rire — *Ici mon cher on ne regarde pas les filles. Par ailleurs, on ne regarde ni les filles et ni les hommes.* Il y a des situations super étranges !¹

— MARC, French
Luxury Industry, New York, U.S.

Peu après mon arrivée, il y avait un homme attendant l'ascenseur. Moi j'étais dedans, seule. Eh bien, l'homme est tout de suite ressorti. Au début, j'ai pensé que je puais, ou que j'avais un problème, car cela s'est reproduit plusieurs fois. J'en ai parlé aux RH. J'ai cru que c'était ma tenue, j'ai pensé qu'il y avait un sujet, je me suis fait plein de films. Alors les H.R. m'ont expliqué ! Je ne pouvais pas y croire.²

— NADINE, French
Finance, New York, U.S.

---

¹ *While arriving at the office, I see a beautiful executive assistant. I look at her for two minutes. The boss saw it. He's laughing his head off—here, my dear, we don't stare at girls. We don't look at girls, and neither do we look at men. There are super weird situations!*

² *Soon after my arrival in the States, there was a man waiting for the elevator. I was in the elevator by myself. Well, the man immediately stepped back out. At first, I thought I stunk or something was wrong with me, because it happened several times. I talked to H.R. about it. I thought it was my outfit, I thought there was an issue. I was obviously overthinking. Then H.R. explained it to me. I couldn't believe it!*

The French have no limits. I struggle with that a lot. I am always afraid my teams will come and complain about misconduct.

— SANDRA, American, living in Paris
HR-Luxury, New York, U.S.

Je voulais faire un mug avec une phrase un peu taquine pour l'anniversaire d'un collègue. On m'a tout de suite conseillé de ne pas le faire. C'est comme ça. Je me bats ici avec notre HR pour comprendre. Il y a des codes. Ils te disent bien que c'est pour éviter des procès. Tout le monde a tout le temps peur.[3]

—MYRIAM, French
FMCG Industry, IL, U.S.

Entre copains, on sait tous *qu'on va se prendre un procès* à un moment ou à un autre… La question, c'est plutôt quand.[4]

—MARC, French
Luxury Industry, New York, U.S.

I lived in France for two and a half years, so I'm used to the French way, but in the U.S., you don't say who you support politically. Now, in my American office, it's very common to hear jokes about Trump, but still, it remains a sensitive subject. The other day, someone said they were going to vote for Trump, and someone else went to HR and complained.

—LAURA, American, lived in Paris
Spirits Industry, New York, U.S.

---

[3] *I wanted to order a mug with a sentence that was a little teasing, for my colleague's birthday. I was immediately advised not to do so. That's just the way it is. I'm struggling here with our HR to figure it out. There are codes. They tell you it's to avoid lawsuits. Everybody is scared all the time.*

[4] *Talking with friends, we all know we're gonna get sued at some point… It's more a question of when.*

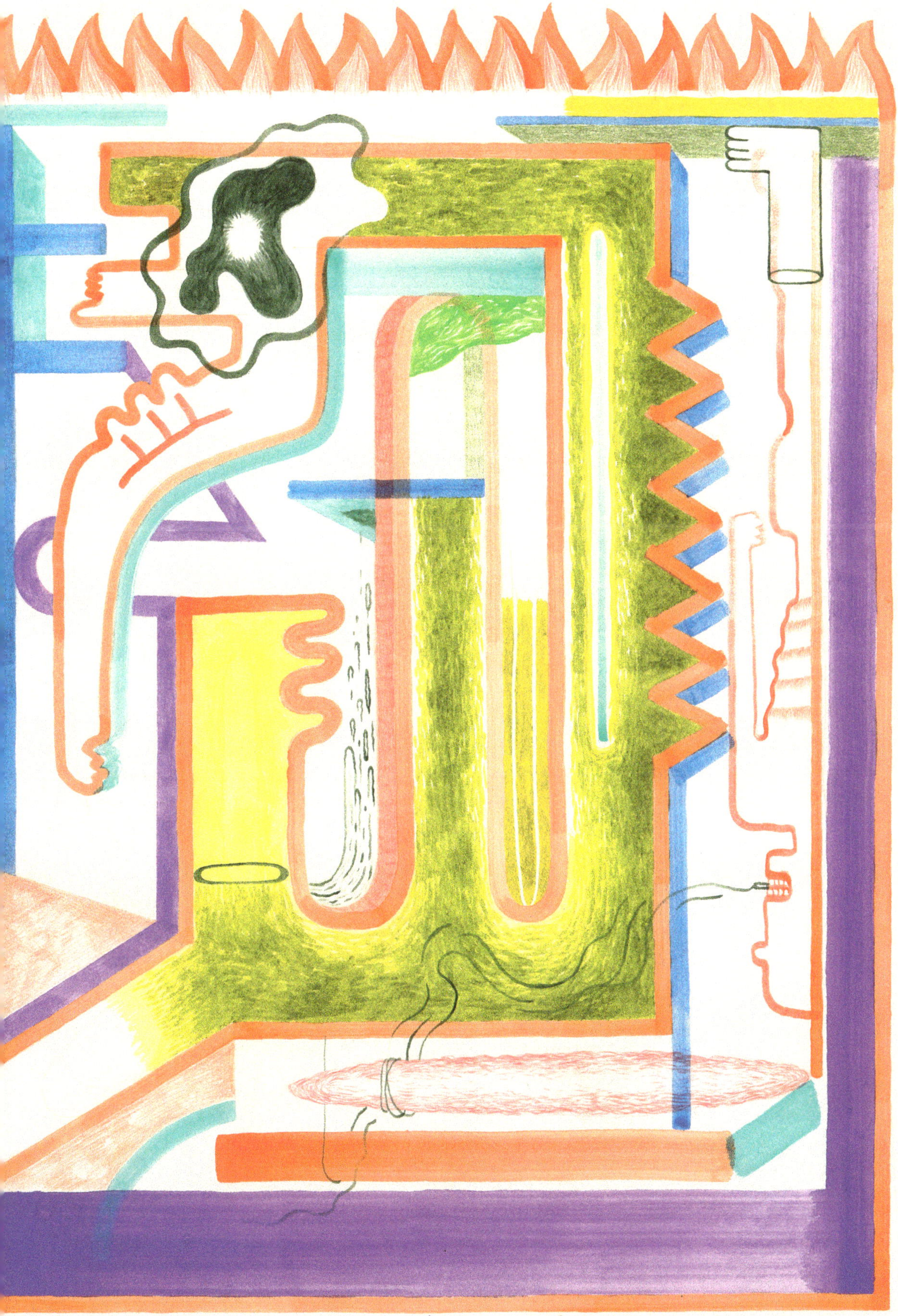

CONCLUSION

For us, working on this book has been a truly eye-opening experience. It helped us revisit our own journey, revealing what we could have done better, faster. It helped us see where we still need to make efforts to truly leverage the best of the two cultures, to develop our curiosity, and grow our understanding.

More importantly, it made us realize how deeply anchored the stereotypes still are, despite the evolutions (generational changes, mobility, and impact of technology).

While our focus for this book was on the symptoms, i.e., the issues and emotions generated by gaps between both cultures, we know these stereotypes are rooted in various deep original factors that might seems stereotypical too, but still extremely important and relevant.

Specifically,

— History: France has a very long history of political and economic transformation, in contrast with the U.S., a land of more recent times. This has fueled two radically different mindsets and cultures that we still see today: one the one side, a mindset of structure, of codes, of reflection, and on the other, pragmaticism, action-solution and fast pace mentality. *Every French person should understand that the U.S. is an immigrant country. We came here with nothing. If you were American at that time, you only had your passion and your desire to achieve things. This optimism is part of the DNA of America even today.* (Louis, French, Health Industry, MA, U.S.) It is the "yes you can" spirit.

— Economy: during decades and even centuries, France has been pioneering social advancements relying on solidarity and state intervention, which means that today, everyone from both the private and public sectors is entitled to health and unemployment coverage. This makes the French workforce less mobile than in the U.S., where people need to rely on themselves, and not on the system, which does not provide a safety net. In the U.S., no work means no insurance! Salaries or bonuses are primarily used to pay off university debts, children's education, retirement programs and medical bills. So the pressure and impact on the role of work is clearly different for that reason too.

— Education: the French system, despite recent transformations, remains very structured, based on individual performance and promoting theory before experience, contrary to the American system, which is all about trial and error, exploration, and group work.

As deep as these differences can be, there is a lot that can be done in order to combat preconceived ideas about each culture. *Because we are a French organization, I tell them they need to immerse into the French culture and learn about it if they want to be happy and succeed here.* (Sandra, American, Luxury Industry [HR position], New York, U.S.)

In the professional context, we realize that there are still numerous opportunities to help organizations embrace this issue more "seriously."

For example, there could be more efficient solutions and incentives to encourage people to learn the language, which remains the first important step toward the other culture. And the solutions currently deployed overall remain somewhat limited. Having a short onboarding program, or being taught the 'scale difference', is not enough!

Without a doubt, there is room for innovation. Corporations, research organizations, professionals and experts could work together to create solutions that would go beyond understanding and anticipating the differences. For example, what if we found an interesting way to trigger a real appetite for the teams to discover the other culture? Not just work-related topics, but even culture in general? Also, what if we found a smart way to encapsulate in a formal way the specific assets of each to truly facilitate mutual education, which we know will not only greatly impact people's performance, but also enhance work satisfaction for everyone? After all, work is about people, motivation, purpose!

Discovering other cultures is a blast. Working in an international context is a chance and a huge opportunity. It should be true in the professional sphere as much as in the personal sphere.

Let's continue the journey of exploring the richness of working together, making sure we understand our differences, accept them, and learn from them to make each of us a stronger professional and a better person.

APPENDIX
—About the French American collaboration

France and the U.S. have a long history of collaboration on political, cultural, and economic levels in particular. Relations between France and America began even before the creation of the United States. The French were among the first to explore the North American coast, settle, and discover the interior!

Today, France and the United States have maintained and developed strong economic ties that are mutually beneficial. This trade and investment promote growth, jobs, and innovation in both countries on a continuous basis. For people, there are many opportunities on both sides to grow their career and discover the richness of working one with another. This is why it is so crucial to understand and respect the cultural differences explained in this book.

Some data help us put things in perspective:

— 160,000 French live in the United States, and some 100,000 Americans live in France
— France is the third largest foreign employer in the United States
— 4,800 French companies employed 678,000 people in the United States in 2017. This makes France the country's third largest foreign employer after the United Kingdom and Japan
— The equivalent of $139 billion worth of goods and services were traded between France and the United States in 2017, a 16% increase over 2016
— In the United States, the states of New York and New Jersey are the two largest importers of French products, and California and Texas are the largest exporters of products to France, particularly in the field of energy
— In 2017, Kentucky imported $2.7 billion in French products—mainly automotive equipment—and Ohio imported $1.68 billion
— The French groups Air Liquide, the world's leading supplier of industrial gas, research, and medicine, and Sodexo, which supplies more than 10,000 food services in the United States, are present in all 50 American states. The insurer Axa is present in 32 states, the automobile equipment manufacturer Michelin in eight states, and the food company Bel in four states
— In 2017, France was the leading foreign job creator in New Jersey and Oklahoma, and French companies created 72,700 jobs in California.

source: https://france-amerique.com/fr/a-french-company-in-every-u-s-state

HIGHLIGHTS

French companies' investment in the U.S.

$129 bn
Trade in goods and services in 2018, up to 7% from 2017

728,500
jobs directly created by French companies investment in the U.S.

50%
of French investment in the U.S. is in the manufacturing sector

30%
of France-U.S. trade in goods is in the aerospace sector

50
All U.S. states trade with France and have some French business presence

$5.6 bn
French companies' R&D expenditures in the U.S. annually

ABOUT THE AUTHORS

Agathe Laurent

Agathe was born in a family with a rich international background, made of stories of immigrations on her maternal side, and on the paternal side, a father who was one of the first in his generation to move to the U.S. for an MBA and start his career there. Only a few months after her birth in Paris, Agathe and her family moved back to the U.S. for a new experience abroad. This became the foundation of her deep aspiration to build herself as a global Citizen of the World and foster her passion for people.

Over time, Agathe cultivated her international flair at every occasion, constantly jumping on a plane for a new adventure, catching a work opportunity abroad, or learning a new language. After a year in Chile helping the underserved, Agathe quickly specialized in Market Research: she realized that studying consumer behaviors, no matter the topic, was an opportunity to learn about people and intercultural differences.

Since then, Agathe has continued to fulfill her passion for connecting with people, and her curiosity for changing cultures. Propelled by her ability to listen, and to analyze, Agathe quickly climbed the ladder in different organizations before launching her own Marketing Consultancy firm, with an office in Paris since 2010 and another in New York since 2018, after 4 years as an SVP at Kantar.

Agathe has been living in New York since 2014 where she raises her three children in a wonderfully bilingual and bi-cultural culture.

Sabine Landolt

Sabine was born on the West Coast as her father, a young chemical engineer, joined the University of California Berkeley. From the San Francisco Bay area, her family transferred to Los Angeles around the UCLA campus. Her family later moved to Lausanne, Switzerland. The Germanophone family had to learn French, including Sabine's Dutch mother. But the American culture had an important presence in the family as her brother decided to move back for his master and for working at Silicon Valley.

"The Polyglot" became Sabine's "personal label." After graduating from the Ecole Supérieure des Arts Appliqués, in Switzerland, Sabine transitioned from the creative world to business development. After a first experience in a Swiss German company, Sabine started moving around the world for what she calls "my professional road trip." Working for well-known multinationals, she was fully immersed in different working styles and management environments. Since then, Sabine has been strongly advocating for how cultural differences impact international business development and human relationships.

Sabine moved her family from Milan to New York where she created a branding boutique agency, dim3branding Inc., and added Canada on her road map while mentoring at McGill University's Entrepreneurship Program in Montreal. Sabine is on the advisory board of Dispersa Inc, a clean tech startup, and co-founded new3plus Inc., a high-end creative makers platform in New York and Sao Paulo, while joining the NEW INC (New Museum incubator).

ARTWORKS CREDITS

Cover	*Untitled,* Bayrol Jimenez, 30 x 42cm, Acrylic paint on paper, 2020
p.14	*Surreal Internet,* Rachel Levit Ruiz, 25 x 25 cm, ink and digital, 2014
p.20	*Sin Título [Untitled],* Diego Beauroyre, 40 x 60 cm, acrylic on canvas, 2019
p.28	*El correo [The email],* Manuel Bueno, 18 x 14 cm, fountain pen on paper, 2017
p.34	*Sin título [Untitled],* Diego Beauroyre, 11 x 14 cm, ink on paper, 2018
p.40	*Sin título [Untitled],* Diego Beauroyre, 28 x 14 cm, indian ink on cotton paper, 2018
p.48	*movimiento y línea IV [movmente and lines IV],* Bayrol Jimenez, 30cm x 42 cm, acrylic paint, color pencils and ink on paper, 2015
p.54	*Café,* Manuela Eguía, 20 x 20 cm, pencil on paper, 2019
p.60	*Torbellino de golpes [Hits Storm],* Antonio Monroy, 21 x 27cm, colored pencils on cotton paper, 2019
p.68	*charcos [puddles],* Bayrol Jimenez, 60 x 80 cm, acrylic paint, color pencils, and ink on paper, 2018
p.74	*Screen light 01,* Alejandro Palomino, 200 x 120cm, charcoal on paper, 2019
p.80	*Pluriverso. Símbolo 4 [Pluriverso. Symbol 4],* Antonio Monroy, 21 x 27 cm, colored pencils on cotton paper, 2019
p.88	*Untitled [Untitled],* Antonio Monroy, 15 x 23 cm, ink on coated paper, 2020
p.94	*Lluvia sobre mojado [Rain on Purple],* Diego Beauroyre, 11 x 14 cm, graphite on paper, 2019
p.101	*cactus calavera [skull cactus],* Bayrol Jimenez, 60 x 80cm, acrylic paint, color pencils, and ink on paper, 2018

CONTRIBUTORS AND THANK YOU

We wanted to express our warmest thank you to all those who helped us bring this project to life, our American and French friends and connections:

Gustave, Mallorie, Valérie, Barbara, Amaury, Alain, Saila, Tracy, Brooke, Jean Christophe, Susan, Anne, Radhika, Tim, Alex, Guillaume, Zoran, Susan, Thierry, Jéremy, Muriel, Brian, Emin, Catherine, Gena, Hyojin, Jan, Louis, Antoine, Danielle, Marie Laurence, Darci, Emmanuel, Jenna, Martine, Nicolas, Charles, Johan, Stephanie, Sylvia, Toni, Caroline, Stephane, Christine, Didier, Thomas, David, Jeff, Jonathan.

We are also very grateful to our friend Anna for her support and time helping us elevate our stories and to our families and numerous friends for their encouragements and unconditional faith in our success.

Thanks to Niha, Sofia and our amazing Lynne, too, for their precious help in the editing, to make our content absolutely perfect.

Thanks to Fabrice, our dear publisher, for trusting us and understanding the meaning of our book immediately!

And last but not least, a big thank you to Surya Son. Her creative eye was such a big plus for translating, for designing the best graphic codes, and reproducing all contents into this amazing contemporary book.

WHY THEY LIKE THIS BOOK

One of the most basic human needs is to understand and be understood. Yet we live in a time when it has become exceeding challenging to fulfill such a need. This book despite its deceiving didactic simplicity offers valuable insights on how to suspend certainties and listen to the other with the intent to understand, not with the intend to judge.

— YOUSSEF MAHMOUD, Former UN Under-Secretary-General, (Senior Advisor at the International Peace Institute)

> La présentation de projets aux équipes américaines et les retours immédiats avec des mots positifs et constructifs participent de leur rayonance. Cette positivité est inclusive et énergique! Le livre de Sabine Landolt et Agathe Laurent est particulièrement inspirant pour trouver ce chemin de l'inclusion et collaboration positive entre des esprits très différents — ceux des Américains et des Français![1]
>
> — DOROTHEE CHARLES, Cultural and Artistic Director Development, Cartier NA

A very original book to explore cultural differences between the French and Americans in a way that I have never seen before! This book is lighthearted and fun but also deep and meaningful. Every French moving to the US for work should read this book, and vice versa. It is lively, original, useful and so human!

— GERARD ARAUD, Ambassador of France to the United States from 2014 to 2019

---

[1] *The presentation of projects to American teams and the immediate feedback embedded with positive and constructive words contribute to their radiance. This positivity is inclusive and energetic! The book by Sabine Landolt and Agathe Laurent is particularly inspiring to find this path of towards inclusion and positive collaboration between very different minds—those of the French and Americans!*

With a thorough, empirical, and dare I say loving approach, Laurent and Landolt show us that differences abound among French and American co-workers, but in the end, there is always a willingness to come together for the greater good. Each nationality recognizes something in themselves, and admires or remarks at least, something unique among their peers in a new shared environment. That seems an excellent foundation on which to build new alliances for the greater good for the business at hand. Surely, more books like this would make a success of international business, creative endeavors and non-profits, alike

— MOLLY BRENNAN, Vice President Sales, International luxury furniture and textiles

> Cet ouvrage très nouveau, fondé sur les expériences réelles de jeunes gens multiculturels d'aujourd'hui, fait le point avec clarté et précision sur les leçons fondamentales qui s'imposent à toute personne cherchant à travailler avec succès en France et aux Etats-Unis. Écrit simplement et intelligemment, il offre de nombreux exemples concrets, dans des contextes variés, qui aideront les lecteurs à naviguer plus à l'aise dans des situations complexes en comprenant les règles du jeu et en évitant les écueils qui pourraient compromettre leur réussite.[2]
>
> — FRANÇOIS RIGOLOT, Meredith Howland Pyne Professor of Literature Emeritus, Princeton University

I am still enjoying dipping my toes into the French American differences pool, finding what would work for me and what wouldn't. As a I am myself originally from Rio de Janeiro but leaving in Sao Paulo, two different cultures in the same country, a book like *Can We Agree to Disagree?* is definitely my cup of tea!

— BERNARDO FARIA, Entrepreneur and Contemporary art Collector, Sao Paulo/New York

---

[2] *This very innovative book, based on real-life experiences of today's multi-cultural people, clearly and precisely outlines the fundamental lessons that are essential for anyone seeking to work successfully in France and the U.S. It is written simply and intelligently, and offers many concrete examples in a variety of contexts: this will help readers navigate more comfortably through complex situations, by understanding the rules of the game and avoiding pitfalls that could jeopardize their success.*

I remain fascinated by this great country and intrigued by the Americans. So close and so far away. Money, sex, religion: we don't laugh at the same jokes and don't take offense at the same flaws. This is what Sabine and Agathe are talking about, with finesse, intelligence, benevolence, humor too. Their book will surprise you, make you smile, certainly think and perhaps spare you some blunders. Must read: on this one at least, can we agree to not disagree?

— PHILIPPE LALLIOT, Current French Ambassador in Dakar, Senegal

Like having a relationship therapist in your pocket! A thoughtful guide to navigating the sometimes choppy waters of French-American relationships; with a focus on the power of empathy.

— KATE GREENE, Global fragrance industry executive and Founder, OUR HOUSE Creative Agency

As an American, I like to focus on action and results, and this book allows take-away steps to make a difference. As a person raised in France, I am sensitive to all things French. I am a true *hybrid* and have used my deep knowledge of both systems and cultures to my advantage throughout my career, and as a *citizen of the world*. The French and American people seem so similar, but the cross-cultural workplace epitomizes many of these dichotomies and differences. A must read for the open minded looking to become better people and more productive at work.

— ELSA BERRY, Managing Director, Vendome Global Partners

I have been through the French cursus par excellence and never thought I would spend such a big part of my professional—and personal obviously—life in the US. Ten years so far, and still counting, over the course of two stays. I have been in more than 40 states. I have supported or joined everything which in one way or another seems transatlantic. I regret nothing of all my past efforts... but this book: had Sabine and Agathe written it earlier I would have saved time and energy and avoided pitfalls and mistakes. Never too late. Thanks to them, I'm getting ready for my next chapter. Merci !

— BERTRAND BADRÉ, CEO Blue like an Orange Sustainable Capital

> La beauté de l'histoire franco-américaine ne saurait gommer les difficultés relationnelles qui naissent parfois de nos différences socio-culturelles. Grâce à une expertise très pragmatique, un ton ludique et bienveillant, ce livre ravive l'enthousiasme à œuvrer ensemble. Frenchies et Yankees ont tant à apprendre les uns des autres ![3]
>
> — FRÉDÉRIQUE BEDOS, Fondatrice de l'ONG d'Information, Le Projet Imagine

This book by Agathe and Sabine offers a practical guide to understanding the working relationships between the French and (North) Americans—especially relevant for professionals working in the province of Quebec, Canada, a culture that is heavily influenced by France. I moved from Toronto to Montreal in 2016, and this book would have been extremely useful in helping me navigate the complexities and dynamics of working with my French colleagues from get-go, rather than learning a lot of the lessons outlined in the book the hard way. Highly recommended reading!

— RENJIE BUTALID, Startup Ecosystem Builder AI Ethics, Entrepreneur, Lecturer McGill University

> The authors lay out and explain through a rich and true-life selection picks of experiences, from both Americans and French sides, very realistic situations. This book pictures not only the immense gap between both cultures, how stereotypes easily lead to misjudgments, and most importantly how urgent it is to drop preconceived ideas. We finally have to admit, that both cultures ways of doing bring tremendous complimentary.
>
> — CLAIRE ISNARD, Global Executive in Fashion&Luxury

In business as in love, any relationship between the French and the American is mined with a potential for misunderstandings and joyous collaboration. Agathe and Sabine have written a practical, engaging guide to happy transatlantic unions.

— MATTHEW KAMINSKI, Editor-in-chief of Politico, co-founder of Politico Europe

---

[3] *The beauty of Franco-American history cannot erase the relational difficulties that sometimes arise from our socio-cultural differences. Thanks to a very pragmatic expertise, a playful and benevolent tone, this book boosts the enthusiasm about working together. Frenchies and Yankees have so much to learn from each other!*

ABOUT TBR BOOKS

TBR Books

A Program of The Center for the Advancement of Languages, Education, and Communities (CALEC)

TBR Books is a program of the Center for the Advancement of Languages, Education, and Communities. We publish researchers and practitioners who seek to engage diverse communities on topics related to education, languages, cultural history, and social initiatives. We translate our books in a variety of languages to further expand our impact. Become a member of TBR Books and receive complimentary access to all our books.

OUR BOOKS IN ENGLISH

Salsa Dancing in Gym Shoes: Developing Cultural Competence to Foster Latino Student Success by Tammy Oberg de la Garza and Alyson Leah Lavigne

Mamma in her Village by Maristella de Panniza Lorch

The Other Shore by Maristella de Panniza Lorch

The Clarks of Willsborough Point: A Journey through Childhood by Darcey Hale

Beyond Gibraltar by Maristella de Panniza Lorch

The Gift of Languages: Paradigm Shift in U.S. Foreign Language Education by Fabrice Jaumont and Kathleen Stein-Smith

Two Centuries of French Education in New York: The Role of Schools in Cultural Diplomacy by Jane Flatau Ross

The Clarks of Willsborough Point: The Long Trek North by Darcey Hale

The Bilingual Revolution: The Future of Education is in Two Languages by Fabrice Jaumont

OUR BOOKS IN TRANSLATION

La Rivoluzione bilingue: Il futuro dell'istruzione in due lingue by Fabrice Jaumont

El regalo de las lenguas : Un cambio de paradigma en la enseñanza de las lenguas extranjeras en Estados Unidos de Fabrice Jaumont y Kathleen Stein-Smith

Rewolucja Dwujęzyczna: Przyszłość edukacji jest w dwóch językach by Fabrice Jaumont

Le don des langues : vers un changement de paradigme dans l'enseignement des langues étrangères aux États-Unis de Fabrice Jaumont et Kathleen Stein-Smith

Our books are available on our website and on all major online bookstores as paperback and e-book. Some of our books have been translated in Arabic, Chinese, English, French, German, Italian, Japanese, Polish, Portuguese, Russian, Spanish. For a listing of all books published by TBR Books, information on our series, or for our submission guidelines for authors, visit our website at

http://www.tbr-books.org

ABOUT CALEC

The Center for the Advancement of Languages, Education, and Communities is a nonprofit organization with a focus on multilingualism, cross-cultural understanding, and the dissemination of ideas. Our mission is to transform lives by helping linguistic communities create innovative programs, and by supporting parents and educators through research, publications, mentoring, and connections.

We have served multiple communities through our flagship programs which include:

– TBR Books, our publishing arm; which publishes research, essays, and case studies with a focus on innovative ideas for education, languages, and cultural development;

– Our online platform provides information, coaching, support to multilingual families seeking to create dual-language programs in schools;

– NewYorkinFrench.net, an online platform which provides collaborative tools to support New York's Francophone community and the diversity of people who speak French.

We also support parents and educators interested in advancing languages, education, and communities. We participate in events and conferences that promote multilingualism and cultural development. We provide consulting for school leaders and educators who implement multilingual programs in their school. For more information and ways, you can support our mission, visit

http://www.calec.org

CPSIA information can be obtained
at www.ICGtesting.com
Printed in the USA
BVHW020153160620
581641BV00016B/991